The Rise of Digital Disruption

A new era of technological advances

The Rise of Digital Disruption

A new era of technological advances

Kerry Quinn

Published by Kerry Quinn Publications

© Copyright Kerry Quinn 2019

THE RISE OF DIGITAL DISRUPTION
A NEW ERA OF TECHNOLOGICAL ADVANCES

All rights reserved.

The right of Kerry Quinn to be identified as the author of this work has been asserted in accordance with the Copyright, Designs and Patents Act 1988.

No part of this publication may be reproduced, stored in a retrieval system, or transmitted, in any form or by any means, electronic, mechanical, photocopying, recording or otherwise, nor translated into a machine language, without the written permission of the publisher.

Condition of sale

This book is sold subject to the condition that it shall not, by way of trade or otherwise, be lent, re-sold, hired out or otherwise circulated in any form of binding or cover other than that in which it is published and without a similar condition including this condition being imposed on the subsequent purchaser.

ISBN 978-1-090-47544-2

Book formatted by www.bookformatting.co.uk.

Contents

Introduction i

Chapter One: The Third Wave 1

    The New Wave of Technology Disruption 1
    Internet 4.0: The Ambient Internet 3

Chapter Two: Business Innovation 6

    SMAC Technology: Driving Business Innovation 6
    Digital Intelligence: Disruption of the C-Suite 9
    Data Analytics for Business Innovation 12

Chapter Three: Change Management 14

    The Rise of the Millennial Workforce 14

Chapter Four: Digital Leadership 18

    Digital Leadership: The Role & Expectations 18
    Organisational Agility: Creating an Agile Environment 20
    The Rapidly Evolving Role of the CMO 21

Chapter Five: Digital Marketing 24

    Client-Agency Relationship: Disruption & Uncertainty 24
    New Rules for Modern Marketers: Data Disruption &
        MarTech 27

Chapter Six: AI & Machine Learning 31

    Leveraging Data, AI and Machine Learning 31
    AI Marketing Analytics 33

Chapter Seven: Digital Strategies 35

    Business Value of APIs 35

Chapter Eight: Digital Transformation 38
  Disruption of Enterprise Architecture 38
  Data Analytics 39
  Digital business transformation objectives & strategies 40
  Transformation Challenges Facing Leaders 43
  The "Digital" in Business Transformation 43
  Considerations for Digital Business Transformation 46
  Worldwide Digital Transformation Predictions 47

Chapter Nine: Emerging Technologies 51
  Human Machine Partnerships 51
  Emerging Technology Trends 52

Chapter Ten: Customer Experience 57
  Innovation & Customer Touchpoints 57

Chapter Eleven: Workforce Evolution 59
  Culture, HR Tools & Remote Working 59
  Unlocking the Benefits of HR Technology Investment 62

Chapter Twelve: Fourth Industrial Revolution 64
  Industry 4.0 64

Notes 68

Bibliography 82
  Note from the author: 95

Disclaimer of Warranty / Limit of Liability

While the author has used their best efforts preparing this book from multiple sources of information across the internet, they make no representation or warranties with respect to the accuracy or completeness of the contents of this book and specifically disclaim any implied warranties or fitness for a particular purpose. No warranty may be created or extended by sales representatives or written sales or marketing material. The advice, opinions and strategies contained herein may not be suitable for your company and or situation. You should consult with a professional when appropriate. Neither the publisher nor author shall be liable for any loss of profit or any other commercial damages, including but not limited to special, incidental, consequential, or other damages. Reference to website URLs in the note section were accurate at the time of writing. Neither the author or the publisher is responsible for changed or expired URLs since the manuscript was prepared.

Acknowledgements

I would like to thank Frank at Book Formatting for his book services and Samantha Signoretto at Designoretto, for her book cover design skills. Special thanks to Susan Quinn, Eileen Thomas, Grace Wilson, Joanne Rees, Alayna Jefferson, Lisa Shaw Jackson, Eunice David, Laura Metcalfe, Simon Tait, Emma Powell, Simon Carr, Andrea Neal, Natalia Lebedenko and Paul Mitchell.

Dedication

In Loving Memory of Andrew.

About the Author

Kerry Quinn is an digital strategist, writer and marketing consultant who hails from Newcastle upon Tyne in the North-East of England. Her experience spans over 20 years' in sales and marketing with 10 years specialising in digital marketing which includes being the founder of a digital marketing agency and training company. She has managed multiple projects across teams and worked on best-in-class marketing communication campaigns.

She has enjoyed being a speaker, trainer and lecturer and trained 100's of business individuals and C-suite executives in the realms of digital strategy and marketing excellence in the UK and Internationally. She has an interest in education, leadership, innovation and enjoys writing on the subject of emerging technologies, marketing and technology disruption.

Introduction

With the digital age disrupting every business and industry, modern marketers, digital strategists and business leaders are gearing up to take their organisations through digital transformation. Disruption and innovation caused by a new era of technology have propelled some companies to success while contributing to the demise of others. Companies that hang on to legacy business models, rigorous regulations, siloed data-sets, drawn-out processes and outdated systems are in danger of their competitor's taken bites out of their market share. Cycles of innovation are occurring exponentially, and companies are struggling to keep up.

The Tech startup sector has also exploded at an unprecedented pace which has resulted in global disruption for our economies. As business models are disrupted by the likes of blockchain and robotics, the creation of IP in other sectors, has created a growing number of sub-sectors. The rise of Deep Tech and the convergence of new technology coined the 'Third Wave' by Gartner is having implications for founders and organisations and paving the way for trends in startup ecosystems and investments, along with funding and talent acquisition opportunities.

Founders are fostering new ways to collaborate and connect with like-minded individuals as they develop quality relationships with each other and local experts. These scaleups and high-performance ecosystems are helping governments and other local leaders, focus their policy and program action plans for greater impact enabling them to deliver national innovation strategies and equip them to understand metrics better to monitor progress on innovations.

THE RISE OF DIGITAL DISRUPTION

Marketing is evolving beyond assumption or creative-driven processes. Driven by intelligent insights and outcomes that focus on customers and the business. Transformation through social, mobile, analytics and cloud technologies gives firms a competitive advantage over the competition while preparing for advancements and challenges for the future digital industry. Modern brands are delivering value by using new technology and informed creativity to engage customers better, improve satisfaction, earn loyalty and grow communities. Businesses are discovering valuable new ways to engage and connect with customers and create new business opportunities to improve existing products, systems, and operations to satisfy consumers connecting with their business through the web, mobile, and social apps.

Digital intelligence is disrupting C-suite executives (CXOs) as they translate digital data into real-time, actionable, customer-centric insights. C-suite roles are evolving with data disruption as they are increasingly involved in technology decisions and purchases, for achieving the next generation of customer experience, (CX) through customer insights (CI). CXOs are turning to the creation of value and new ways of working in an agile environment. They are looking at the restructuring of people, processes, technology, strategies and moving away from managerial hierarchy structures. With the rise of globalisation, remote and flexible working, the teamwork landscape is changing resulting in a global workforce evolution.

The rise of disruptive technologies have redefined IT capabilities and thrust the industry into transformative change. Employees now have access to workforce tools which has changed the world of work and technological dexterity in the consumer products market has given rise to wide-ranging analytical processing power, growth in data and increasingly shorter technology lifecycles.

Where once the role of a marketer was traditionally communication and campaign-focused. The position has now been disrupted by technology and compliance as they deal with a myriad of complexities of acquiring, understanding, translating, and leveraging data from an infinite amount of devices, platforms and channels. New

INTRODUCTION

challenges in data sensitivity and compliance surrounding GDPR, attribution modelling, cross-device identity, understanding the marketing and technology landscape has reverberated marketers in a formidable way.

Digital leadership is one of the most sought-after skill sets in many organisations. We're seeing a rise in organisations of all shapes and sizes embarking on digital transformation – a term that's synonymous with undertaken an overhaul of traditional processes with the adaption of a digital-front-end.

By 2050, 60% of the population is expected to live in cities. Cities are digitally transforming to improve environmental, financial, and social aspects of urban life and city technology spending is said to be expected to grow to $135 billion by 2021, according to the International Data Corporation (IDC). The term 'smart cities' is no longer viewed as a trend. Smart cities are defined as using data and technology to create efficiencies, improve sustainability, create economic development, and enhance the quality of life factors for people living and working in a city.

Civilisation is on the verge of the next industrial revolution which is called 'Industry 4.0'. A term used to refer to the developmental process in the management of manufacturing and chain production. It represents a significant transformation regarding the way we produce products by the digitisation of manufacturing and a new wave of technological change which is enabling factories and warehouses to transform.

This book is an exploration into how technology is transforming industries and how business leaders, marketers and organisations are responding to disruption to grow in a thriving age of digitalisation. It seeks to explore the paradigm shift in business, society and the drivers behind digital business transformation and change management.

Chapter One: The Third Wave

The New Wave of Technology Disruption

Disruption is taken place on an industry-wide scale, forcing a significant shift in business models. Technological changes have changed business logic through digital innovation and practices, products, and services have evolved and fundamentally altered the strategy of companies. A new model typically provides customers with the same or better value. Companies that stick to old business models could lose market share, and some could face being pushed out of business. Leaders that embrace new business models gain advantage and can result in claiming a dominant position in the market.

During the next few years, technologies associated with the third wave such as robotics, artificial intelligence, cloud computing, online interface design, Internet of Things (IoT), Industry 4.0, cyberwarfare, and data analytics will advance and boost overall impact on one another and streamline and improve business operations. Products and processes will learn from their surroundings and markets will converge to an unprecedented extent. This new wave of technological advance is expected to alter a wide array of business practices, in nearly every sector, in both business-to-business and business-to-consumer companies.

Preparations for these changes require time, and the precise tipping point will vary from one industry to the next. Some common threads will emerge such as price decrease, loss of assets value, and change in customer habits will determine the pace of change. Disruption will, eventually, reach its destination but in the early stages of technological advance, it may seem as though nothing is happening. However, if you've already started to prepare, you'll be ready for it by the time the shift occurs. To respond effectively companies are seeking people with software and development skills such as DevOps to help them reinvent and change business models.

Digital technology reduces operational costs when applied strategically and innovatively. Business models find new ways to meet customer demand, one that adds convenience or provides value. Disruptions are different in several ways and involve technologies that can reduce the need for physical assets. Value chains and markets are reshaping, rendering the old differences among sectors irrelevant. It affects a broad number of industries, as companies add scale with digital platforms and APIs which enables them to launch new and improved products and services.

Technology enables companies to do more with assets that were underutilised before. Technology drives scale, and scale drives profitability. Cloud computing, employee remote-work opportunities are becoming popular. Reliance on assets explains why some companies hold on for so long to their old legacy models. As disruptive companies deliver improved value in all these ways, and customers come on board, old customer habits erode slowly.

When a tipping point is reached, and revenues and purchases move to new models and gain momentum, customers notice how easy and beneficial it will be for them to switch. Soon after, the remaining majority shift suddenly, and the industry follows. From there, it may take just months until old business models are no longer sustainable.[1] Disruption typically takes one of two forms either, the new model completely replaces the old, or the new and old business models coexist. Some legacy companies adapt modestly to the modern world and find ways to keep attracting new customers.

The third wave is described as being the stage where all companies are internet-powered tech companies, and any newcomers will challenge the biggest incumbent industries in the world (think Uber and Airbnb). New companies will join forces with third parties, like established firms and especially government regulators. The three rules of the Third Wave are partnerships, policy and perseverance.[2]

INTRODUCTION

A new wave of internet startups are disrupting established businesses by the process of decoupling which is described as the separation of two or more activities ordinarily done in conjunction by consumers. Digital disruptors can have a substantial negative impact on traditional businesses as they are changing the way consumers entertain themselves, shop, communicate with others and even own products. As such, companies will need to rethink their monetisation strategies and either recouple consumer activities or rebalance the revenues generated from each business activity.[3]

Conclusion: The wave of digital disruption will have far-reaching effects across many different industries. Digital technology has already shown its ability to outpace efforts to control it. Many partial disruptions could continue perpetually starting as partial disruption and end up moving into total or near-total disruption. The future of enterprises will depend on how well leaders understand the dynamics in their industry and in general the impact of digital disruption. The constraint for a company will not be the technology; it will be the ability to lower costs, engage customers effectively, and make better use of assets to streamline processes. A business that employs digital technology to do all three together effectively, will be among the successors of the age of digital disruption.

Internet 4.0: The Ambient Internet

We have seen the Internet go through different stages of growth through advances in technology, and we're now embarking on a revolutionary set of changes that makes the network ambient and its fluidity is simplifying life. Internet 4.0 is embedded in various devices that we use on a daily basis and is accessible for everyone in our interconnected digital world. The intelligence behind some technology is that of voice recognition and assistance — Amazon's Alexa, Apple's Siri, Google's OK... Google or Microsoft's Cortana - employs examples, to execute tasks. The emergence is visible yet invisible at the same time, and digital skills are seemingly no longer a prerequisite with some applications.[4] Internet 1.0: The pre-web

THE RISE OF DIGITAL DISRUPTION

Internet, dates back to 1968-1995 when the Internet was an unknown phenomenon and the focus was on sharing computing resources and exchanging information. Internet 2.0: (Rise of the Web) came about In the 1995-mid 2010s and saw the appearance of the web democratised. The web era allowed for access to communication tools so that anyone could set up their presence online and compete in the online world. Web 2.0: (The Social Web) is where social media platforms such as Facebook became the dominant player for daily social life while LinkedIn established itself as the professional networking site.

Internet 3.0: (The Mobile Internet) started in 2008- until the present day with the introduction of the Apple app store. It marks the mobile Internet era- iPhones and app stores. The app store model disrupted the Internet as it fundamentally changed how people interacted with the Internet. As new business models were created to leverage the mobility of devices, it also opened the floodgates for infrastructure to make the Internet more available on a continuous basis through mobile devices and massive amounts of data about usage.[5]

The Ambient Internet (2017-future), with mobile devices now a majority of Internet traffic, the Ambient Internet is taking information based on where your device has been and combining that with information that is coming off nearby sensors and adding artificial intelligence to drive new experiences that are embedded into existing devices. The Internet will move from specific devices such as mobile phones or computers to interfaces that interact naturally. Early representatives of this trend are home assistants like Amazon Alexa and Google Home. Historical data is gathered through interactions with multiple touchpoints and merges it with contextual information collected through wearable sensors or installed nearby, and uses Artificial Intelligence to establish what you are most likely to need.

Conclusion: The future of Internet 4.0 is the state of ambient computing it creates through natural interactions, either via spoken dialogue or text embedded into tools already used in messaging pro-

INTRODUCTION

grams. Internet 4.0 is about driving a personalised Internet with products and services to please the majority of the people in that location. The final stage of the Ambient Internet is Internet penetration that will lead to the Internet disappearing in the background. Thus, it is rapidly becoming a core service that connects to everything around us.

Chapter Two: Business Innovation

SMAC Technology: Driving Business Innovation

Over the past few years, we've seen a new wave of IT technology known as the SMAC stack- a holistic solution and concept that social, mobile, analytics and the cloud that has changed the face of enterprise IT which is driving business innovation. SMAC technology has accelerated enterprise-level digital transformation causing industries to rethink their digital strategies. The rise of disruptive technologies have redefined IT capabilities and thrust industries into transformative change. SMAC is arguably the foundation for doing business in a digital economy, where data analytics and information technologies are the basis for new business models and giants such as Amazon, Facebook and Netflix are examples of business models of excellence in this new world order.

SMAC technology is also revolutionising the workplace-enabling businesses to transition from an e-business to a digital company. Employees now have access to a myriad of workforce tools which has changed the world of work and technical skill in the consumer products market that has given rise to wide-ranging analytical processing power, growth in data and increasingly shorter technology lifecycles.

SMAC technologies are the change agents in enterprise IT as they make it possible for businesses to create future-proof digital work environments that cut costs, enhance and improve operations, bringing companies closer to their customers and improving employee performance and customer experience.[1]

Today, business models are reshaped by SMAC technology, not

only because they help companies develop and deliver their products and services from customer-generated data, but also the role that technology plays in the operations of organisations across all industries. The integration of social, mobile, analytics and cloud together creates a competitive advantage and new business opportunities with hyper-intelligent software platforms.

IT in the workplace has evolved, so too has consumer technology products in people's personal lives with the evolution of Smart Homes, Smart Cities, IoT, AI, wearables etc. Employees now expect the same innovative quality and ease of use with enterprise technology at work. SMAC technologies are digitally transforming businesses to be better equipped for the future. When implemented seamlessly together in the SMAC stack, the convergence of these four technologies serves as a holistic solution for digital transformation.[2]

Social technologies enable quick sharing and creation of knowledge over social networks such as Twitter, Facebook, Instagram and Snapchat which enhances collaboration and information distribution across a business providing businesses with new ways to reach, interact with, target and acquire customers. People are the most valuable asset of any organisation, and social technologies help harness and facilitate the dissemination of individuals knowledge to drive business results.

Mobile technologies are reshaping the technology landscape and have ultimately changed the way people communicate, shop and work. Businesses on board with mobile technologies are reaping the benefits and with the introduction of connected devices and wearable devices are being offered to customers.

Big Data analytics allows businesses to deconstruct and understand how, when and where people consume goods and services, which generates unprecedented insight enabling decision making in real time. Analytics enhances supply chains, help to predict future customer behaviour, and makes closed-loop marketing easier while optimising existing customer relationships.

Cloud is the new foundation of the IT ecosystem as it provides the data needed for a business to respond to changing markets and solve business problems quickly. Cloud computing lends businesses newfound agility, breaking down the barriers of geography and cutting the costs associated with physical server maintenance. Amazon Web Services is one of the first big disruptors in this space with its seemingly limitless scalability.

The International Data Corporation (IDC), identified a shift to the 3rd Platform of cloud, mobile, big data, analytics and social, which dominated industry revenues. The IDC states The Innovation Accelerators will drive the next wave of 3rd Platform growth, resulting in the 3rd Platform accounting for 75% of ICT spending by 2021. These innovation accelerators include IoT, cognitive AI, robotics, AR/VR, 3D printing, and next-gen security.[3]

However, Gartner identifies the convergence of mobile, social, cloud and information as being a 'Nexus of Forces' for a digital business. Gartner also coined the term bimodal IT in 2014, which is a "two-tiered operations model that enables IT to divide tasks into two modes: processes that are stable, sequential and slow and processes that require an Agile and iterative approach needed to develop digital products and services".[4] Furthermore, at The Open Group, they refer to the convergence as 'Open Platform 3.0™'. The 'Open Group Open Platform 3.0 Forum' focuses on new and emerging technology trends converging with each other and leading to new business models and system designs. The 'Internet of Things' or IoT is the intelligence that makes products and services smarter, and some believe it belongs under the SMAC umbrella.[5]

SMAC allows for social media activities to better reach and interact with larger customer segments. Mobile technologies change the way people communicate and interact with each other giving insights into the customer minds through mobile apps. Analytics tracks opinions and preferences allowing businesses to deeply analyse and understand customer behaviour and their response patterns better. Cloud computing provides new ways to access technology anywhere, anytime making it possible for businesses and customers to access the data in these ever-changing markets. Such technologies are causing a paradigm shift in business models across business verticals helping to identify new market segments and deliver agility, scalability and context driven marketing initiatives. DevOps are developing software and digital products and services.

Conclusion: SMAC technology is a concept that makes use of social interactions, mobility, analytics-driven by big data and cloud technology to simplify the customer experience while boosting productivity. Digital transformation prioritises the end-user experience, setting the right strategy for businesses to deploy a tailored and holistic SMAC solution. The increasing frequency of disruption presents several challenges that bring distinct stressors; but also offer a platform for potential growth and business innovation. They help an organisation to unify data and processes, improve digital capabilities, make better decisions through data analytics and transform businesses with IT integration and solution delivery.

Digital Intelligence: Disruption of the C-Suite

Digital intelligence is disrupting the C-suite and CXOs (collective term for C-suite executives) are gearing up to translate digital data into real-time, actionable, customer-centric insights in today's data-driven world. Roles are evolving with data disruption as they are increasingly involved in technology decisions and purchases, for achieving the next generation of customer experience, (CX) through customer insights (CI). The CMO of Dun and Bradstreet in an Adobe article states that data is the foundation on which an entire business is built and without accurate, structured and shared data sets across an organisation, decisions will continue to be made in silos and valuable resources will continue to be wasted as information is outdated or simply incorrect. Therefore, every c-level executive needs to know the data strategy for their company in a fast-paced digital environment.[6]

According to Forrester; Insights-driven businesses have an edge on their competitors as digital intelligence practices synchronise digital analytics with digital interactions to continuously deliver optimised customer experiences at scale. They suggest that it's time for customer insights professionals to follow suit and work with teams across the enterprise to foster a mature intelligence practice capable of competitive differentiation.[7]

An insights report, states that organisations with a cross-team approach with their customers at the heart of all initiatives and nearly twice as much likely to have exceeded their top business goal by a significant margin. Furthermore, as companies continue to focus on the customer experience they will outperform their peers. Just under two-thirds of companies agree that they have a cohesive plan, long-term view and executive support for their future customers. Top strategic priorities include content and experience management and almost half of companies surveyed rank this as one of their three most important priority areas.[8]

Research carried out by MIT Sloan Management Review, suggests that a company's digital intelligence is informed by four dimensions: strategy, culture, organisation, and capabilities.[9]

Traditionally, the C-suite includes a Chief Marketing Officer (CMO), Chief Information Officer (CIO), Chief Financial Officer (CFO) and Chief Operations Officer (COO), who collectively work closely with the Chief Executive Officer (CEO) to manage the marketing, operations, finance and information systems to keep the company running successfully. However, there is now a shift toward creating leadership roles that focus entirely on the customer experience – supported by data.

The expansion of the new C-suite includes the following job titles:

Chief Customer Officer (CCO), a leader that provides the comprehensive and authoritative view of the customer and creates corporate and customer strategy at the highest levels of the company to maximise customer acquisition, retention, and profitability.

Chief Data Officer (CDO), is involved in risk, compliance, policy management, and business role. They serve to drive information and analytics strategy.

Chief Digital Officer (CDO), started as a focus on the digital customer experience is now reaching into corporate strategy, innovation, technology and operations.

Chief Analytics Officer (CAO), leads data analytics strategy, driving data-related business changes to transform the business into a more analytics-driven one.

Chief People Officer (CPO), the highest ranking of the Human Resources ladder, responsible for staff and culture (values, ethics, mission), and creates a working environment in which employees can thrive.

All additional hybrid roles now sit within the C-suite of an enterprise for digital business transformation. Some may argue that successful digital intelligence is due to every person involved in marketing and the role that Artificial Intelligence will play in the customer journey. Digital intelligence tools are certainly giving CXOs the ability to truly understand how their customers are using their website or mobile app through data insights and transferring data intelligence into strategies to optimise the customer experience. Digital intelligence is here to stay, and organisations are restructuring as they acknowledge and become aware of changes in their industry, customer expectations and employee perspectives. When it comes to digital, CXOs are relying on technology to equip them in the business landscape and improve customer experience. The goal of digital intelligence is to create a faster, smarter and better business that can anticipate and meet its customers' needs. From artificial intelligence to machine learning, cloud platforms such as Adobe Experience Cloud and software-as-a-service modelling – digital information can help reduce spend and increase revenue. More importantly, It can increase customer engagement and empower customers toward a more meaningful customer journey.

Conclusion: Digital intelligence can help CXOs chart a clear and strategic customer journey to have the edge over competitors. The underpinning of digital transformation is about successfully integrating technology into business to meet and exceed the expectations of today's consumers to ensure they become tomorrow's loyal advocates. That involves both a clear customer experience vision and commitment to data intelligence for informed decision making. Digital knowledge enhances customer loyalty, increases sales, improves efficiencies, and creates value. Businesses need the right leaders who are committed to its vision and work with teams across the entire organisation.

Data Analytics for Business Innovation

Companies are gaining competitive advantage from their use of data and analytics for reasons, including wider use of analytics as well as a stronger focus on specialised, innovative applications that have strategic benefits. Innovation from analytics is surging with the growing use of data and analytics and organisations with strong analytics capabilities are using those abilities to innovate not only existing operations but also new business models, processes, products and services. Data governance to foster innovation as companies share data internally and beyond company boundaries, resulting in more value from their analytics which enables data governance practices for innovation. However, to be effective, data governance needs to be embedded in an organisation's culture and it must actually influence organisational behaviour.

Smart machines create opportunity for innovative thinking as they draw from data and learn by using algorithms to discern patterns in masses such as speech recognition. Artificial intelligence is being used to augment human skills for time-consuming tasks which are freeing managers to spend more time on strategic development. Analytical Innovators are companies that adopt an analytics culture and make data-driven decisions based on analytics for strategic insights and innovative ideas. Analytics can be used for operational improvements and companies that are not advanced rely on management intuition than data for decision making which results in lack of data management skills. The ability to innovate with data is tied to effective data-sharing practices yet in many organisations, data remains stuck in silos within departments. Technical barriers to sharing are eroding with increased reliance on infrastructure such as cloud computing, but organisational barriers are still common impediments to dissolving data silos and creating broad-based access to useful information. Many functional areas within organisations increasingly look to data and analytics as a source of knowledge and influence. As more companies use analytics for a competitive edge and more departments explore the potential of analytics, several complementary trends are emerging.

Businesses are taking data seriously by viewing data as an organisational asset with strong data governance practices and are not relying exclusively on its own data. Data from other organisations can give insights around customer behaviour and market segmentation. Executives should weigh the trade-offs that come with developing an in-house capability for integrating and analysing datasets. Creating processes that result in data confidence is critical.

Conclusion: Data sharing requires departments to work together, sometimes with other organisations to create mechanisms for understanding how other business silos use data. Cultural norms that encourage executives to use these mechanisms are critical as data sharing delivers business value. To be effective, they need to be embedded in the culture of the organisation. Data sharing will vary depending on what industry a company is in and how heavily regulated that industry is. Innovating with data means ensuring that functional areas have the data and analytics capabilities to apply data to specific business problems. This involves democratising access to data, to gain an advantage through analytics.

Chapter Three: Change Management

The Rise of the Millennial Workforce

Millennials' have a positive impact on change management as they help transform the way business thinks, works and deals with challenges. According to PwC millennials form 25% of the US workforce and account for over half of the population in India. By 2020, millennials will form 50% of the global workforce. So it's no surprise that a lot has been written about this generational group regarding the impact they have on change management and how their leadership style and corporate culture affects business transformation programs.[1]

Millennials hold about 20% of all leadership roles and Millennial leaders prioritise values, ethics, flexibility, and feedback. They're about to define a new generation of leadership and influence.[2]

Millennials would prioritise the sense of purpose around people rather than growth or profit of an organisation.[3] Millennials are in every way the game-changers or path-breakers who can show the way ahead. From leading innovation to driving changes, this generation is a shining example of revolution and transformation. Time must be taken to embrace their values and culture to make businesses better.[4]

Resistance to change is a common challenge for any change management program as change management professionals meet the demands and expectations of both internal and external stakeholders as well as manage the direct impact that change has on organisational structure, business processes, systems, scalability, technology and resistance by the workforce. Some organisations are pairing top management with younger employees in a programme of 'reverse mentoring' to help managers put themselves in younger employees' shoes and to coach executives in IT, social media and the latest workplace trends. Workplace mentors used to be higher up the ranks (and older) than their mentees however this is no longer the case as social media skills become increasingly valuable. These programmes also help to transfer corporate knowledge to millennials, which will become increasingly important as Baby Boomers retire in greater numbers.[5]

Baby Boomers and Generation X-ers have historically adhered to a top-down corporate structure. However, A downward flow is considered to be outdated and inefficient to millennials. Instead, millennials prefer collaboration tools that invite a two-way medium which impacts the methods and tools organisations use to communicate around change. Millennials thrive on newfound goals and challenges to keep them motivated: new products, new campaigns, or a new organisational chart.[6]

Millennials receive and access information on mobile devices more than any other medium. The average millennial spends an average 18 hours consuming media daily and they touch their smartphone 43 times and spend roughly 5.4 hours of that total on social media. So, whatever the channel the likelihood is that a millennial will consume information on a mobile device which has implications for the content as well as the formatting of the messaging that is sent out such as shorter, more concise messaging with interactive features. Therefore, a comprehensive mobile strategy should be front-of-mind when considering communications for any change management project.[7]

Technology is second nature to this tech-savvy generation group as they expect tools to keep pace as they work comfortably and adapt quickly to changes in an agile environment – making them a robust solution and business transformation enablers. The rise of the millennial workplace and the increase in management roles, change management professionals are becoming increasingly aware of the way in which this evolution is reshaping traditional structures. The needs and work habits of millennials are essential factors in how change initiatives are considered. The effects of generational change mean that change management professionals are learning how to harness this transformational force.

Millennials in leadership roles are not interested in the number of hours their staff are spending behind a desk. They would instead give workers as much flexibility as they can as long as they do their job. Resulting in more organisations having to introduce more flexible and remote working schedules. This environment poses a challenge to change management practices. Those who are involved in organisational transformations need to consider remote working. The strategy for managing change for a millennial workforce remains true to change management principles, albeit there is no one-size-fits-all approach. Four areas that could be key to the success of any change effort involving millennials are communication types, learning and development, training and employee engagement platforms.[8]

Communication Types:

- Consistent, open and honest communication is important
- A mobile strategy can help ensure communications are mobile
- Messaging should be short, crisp and to-the-point and interactive

Learning and Development:

- Appetite to develop and enhance their skill set
- A holistic perspective of various business units
- Open to exploring new avenues/verticals

Flexible and On-Demand Training:

- Thirst for on-the-go nano- learning
- Reluctant to want to learn in a classroom environment
- Role-based training modules

Employee Engagement Platform:

- Focus on year-round engagement
- Want to feel empowered by suggesting ideas
- Platform to build each employee's sense of purpose
- Proactive engagement practices to motivate

Conclusion: There is no doubt that Millennials are 'trailblazers'. They quickly adapt to leading technology and are quick to discover and implement resourceful approaches that boost company productivity. Millennials values, expectations, and demands will continue to shape the future of work as they bring newer perspectives and more innovative approaches to the table. Millennials want to make a difference and seek a company culture that has a positive impact on society. Companies would do well to learn how to harness their contributions and recognise the real potential they possess. Millennials want to be incentivised and be informed about changes their organisation is undergoing, and information should be presented in a format they prefer interacting with while playing a significant role in the transformation journey.

Chapter Four: Digital Leadership

Digital Leadership: The Role & Expectations

Digital leadership is one of the most sought-after skill sets in many organisations across the globe today. Consumers are transforming and adapting to new ways to engage and purchase faster than ever before. Therefore, companies are now looking for people with "digital leadership" qualities that can drive innovation and understand how technology is transforming consumers and society, and be able to translate this into business impact. CEOs require strong digital leaders to champion digital transformation change within their company's structure and strategy and improve the customer experience.The role of the CMO has changed from being *"once the leader responsible for creativity and brand, today's CMO has vast and complex responsibilities reaching far beyond traditional marketing — now spanning technology, analytics, growth and, above all, measurable impact"*.[1] What are the traits of a successful digital leader? Research shows that it is someone who inspires and educates. A willingness to undergo digital transformation and understand 'big-data', content marketing, social selling and can genuinely create innovative ideas to ensure the business evolves with future changes. Digital leaders foster a collaborative environment, breaks down silos and are willing to take risks and develop new capabilities and attract talent. Successful digital leaders are ones who are always visible and communicate regularly.

DIGITAL LEADERSHIP

The role of a digital leader:

- Set the vision
- Influence executives and stakeholders
- Create sustainable digital programs
- Hire A players
- Define processes for digital excellence
- Track impact
- Optimise and continually improve

What are the characteristics of an effective digital leader?

- Someone who leads
- Inspires
- Educates
- Enables
- Empowers
- Fosters partnerships
- Accountable

What skills do digital leaders need? Digital leaders are required to improve corporate performance which often involves lots of initiatives aimed at boosting revenue, cutting costs, or both during transformation phases. Key skills are motivating and influencing others and delegating work. Strong team leadership isn't enough, new research shows the importance for business impact and career success as well as being able to mobilise your boss and colleagues.[2]

Digital leaders are willing to transform and embrace the digital world. They recognise a need to become digitally fluent and integrate digital thinking into everyday management and encourage employees to develop digital competencies. The more digitally literate a workforce, the greater their potential to contribute to value creation, foster new relationships with customers and employees and understand the shifts; behavioral, economic and social factors that new technology drivers create.[3]

It is stated that *"The truly disruptive leader doesn't need to talk about disruption because it's simply how they get things done."* The most dynamic leaders are said to be relentless in pursuing the truth, guide others' through chaos, are decisive, give explanations when they rewrite and break rules and thrive in times of uncertainty.[4]

Conclusion: Digital leaders are required to improve corporate performance aimed at boosting revenue, cutting costs or both during digital transformation phases. Digital leaders have the health and prosperity of a company as their top priority. They embrace technology and innovation and make sure this is part of the company culture as they build lean internal processes to gain the flexibility to utilise the brightest internal and external talent.

Organisational Agility: Creating an Agile Environment

Organisations are adapting to the demands of new technology, competition and consumer ecosystems to create organisational agility. CXOs are turning to the creation of value and new ways of working in an agile environment. Organisations are looking at the restructuring of people, processes, technology, strategies and moving away from managerial hierarchy structures. Agility needs two things. One is the capability of being dynamic so that companies can be responsive and move at speed. The second is stability and a foundation that does not transfer to enable a springboard effect and bring a level of confidence to be agile. So in essence; Companies can become agile by designing their organisations to drive both speed and create stability.[5]

Regulations in large established companies can stifle agility as there are a more significant number of policies, rules and complex management structures. Whereas, start-ups, can act quickly in the beginning up to a certain point and then may struggle at a certain size or scale without stability. However, with globalisation and disruptors entering industry markets, it is paramount for any size or maturity of a company to be agile and respond to change.

Another interesting notion during the same interview states: "You have to reduce the structure, the processes", and suggests that leaders should take things away instead of adding structures, processes and rules as seen in an all too familiar managerial hierarchy.

> "The first responsibility of a leader is to define reality. The last is to say thank you. In between, the leader is a servant."
> – Max De Pree

In an agile environment, the role of a manager is to ensure value for the customer. For this to happen, people's talent and contributions should be fluid. So the role of a manager is reversed to that of an enabler. As consumers lead the way – changing company culture and ideology at the top-layers is more beneficial to the customer and thus more profitable for companies. This can be achieved through the persuasion of managers to stop acting like a boss. Instead, implement leadership storytelling, focusing on delivering value to customers while embracing an outside-in approach instead of top-down or bottom-up.[6]

Conclusion: accomplishing organisational agility is not going to be easy for some senior managers. A company's culture will have embedded a set of rules, plans, principles, attitudes and assumptions for many years. Breaking that mould is going to be a tough leadership challenge. However, it can be reached by work not being conducted by bureaucracy, and rather, work cycles should be iterative with direct feedback from the customer. Continuous improvements and transparency in self-organising teams are at the heart of successful organisational agility.

The Rapidly Evolving Role of the CMO

The role of the Chief Marketing Officer is evolving faster than any other CXO, and all eyes are on them to lead the way in a new marketing world. Today's CMO has moved from traditional to technology, analytics, growth, ROI, P&L, and leads a department as well as earning a seat at the C-suite table. They bring a unique set of skills to drive a business forward- juggling a multitude of complex issues with data scientists on their team.[7]

CMOs oversee multiple markets, restructure operational marketing models so that business units can align to ensure the customer experience journey is streamlined within a new brand interfacing ecosystem. They consider talent acquisition, the adoption of new tools and processes to achieve brand and business change which in turn, provides a path for true and impactful digital transformation. However, above all, CMOs need to be able to measure impact and shape business objectives.

A Deloitte survey of 300 CMOs found that marketing leaders have seen their function change significantly over the last five years, creating gaps between what marketers now expect and what agencies are delivering. The biggest of these gaps is in the area of data analytics and two-thirds of CMOs are using analytics to make key decisions, however, they recognise that they're not close to realising the full potential of their data. It's a brand new marketing world and all eyes are on the CMO to lead the way as they are valued as strategic advisors for their increasing knowledge of customers, markets, competition – and expectations to deliver results.[8]

Key findings of the report include:

- 89% saying that marketing has changed radically over the past five years;
- 75% see their role as increasingly influential to the business success;
- 80% feeling increased expectations;
- 71% recognising data analytics as their most significant challenge;
- 82% say the problem to transform and acquire new skills is increasing.

As companies advance to becoming a digital-first business,

CMOs are transforming the customer experience by working collectively with IT, sales, customer service and product management. A biannual survey found that digital dominates when it comes to corporate marketing budgets. Survey respondents-95.3% of whom are VP level or above, are allocating more dollars than ever to digital and expect to spend a full 54% of marketing budgets on digital within the next five years (upto 2023). Digital advertising continues to outperform with a growth rate of 12.3% compared to traditional which is slipping -1.2%. The Survey of 324 top marketing leaders at U.S. for-profit companies was conducted between July and August 2018, from a pool of 2,895 and was based on marketing spending. Unsurprisingly, this highlights the need for CMOs to work together with Chief Digital Officers to drive digital transformation.[9]

Conclusion: New technologies, tools and market dynamics are fast moving and redefining the job specification of the Chief Marketing Officer. With the rising importance of the use of data analytics to generate customer insights, Chief Marketers will need to work closely with data science teams and IT. They will embrace a learning culture of change to understand how emerging technologies and data insights can enable growth. They will play a leadership role in data analytics, customisation, personalisation, and optimisation, to drive highly targeted, sophisticated, complex, digital-led campaigns and activities. They will form strategic partnerships with the CEO to offer up their deep knowledge of customers to bring products and services to the market.

Chapter Five: Digital Marketing

Client-Agency Relationship: Disruption & Uncertainty

Transformation of the client-agency relationship is prevalent as brands look to bring agency work in-house. Agencies are only as good as the people leading them, and the failure of agencies to show ROI, globalisation and the rise of procurement have all played a part in this new in-house phenomena in an overcrowded and over-supplied space. According to the Digital Marketing Institute (DMI), only 23% of employees have the digital capabilities required to achieve business outcomes and 40% of organisations are unable to find sufficient talent to handle their digital marketing workloads. 70% of large companies say their digital marketers are strong in some areas but weak in others.[1]

Successful agencies will invest in marketers who adapt to AI, and machine learning automation technology – enabling them to transform, interpret data and figure out the best customer experience approach in moments of adversity. Agencies would benefit from more of an agile approach to accommodate project-based assignments and refrain from retainer pricing models. They most certainly need to be realistic about the capabilities of their marketing team as some marketers are just dipping their toes into a vast world of data while being in a constant phase of testing and iteration.[2]

Agencies are hired for a whole host of services however, brands are now seeing the value of hiring data-scientists and bringing in digital transformation/management consultants who can come straight into the inner workings of their company and make an immediate impact. Historically, agencies have owned the skills-set of UX design, creativity, customer-centric data analytics and customer engagement but that's all changing as brands look to improve the experience their customers receive across multi-channels in real-time.

Every business needs to evolve, and the same goes for agencies to keep the client-agency relationship going as brands take back control over their operations, data, advertising and marketing capabilities. Agencies are competing with management consultants who are already skilled at smaller assignments and understand complex marketing ecosystems. Agencies who consider transforming their operations, investing in technology, upskilling or hiring specialist talent to deal with the demand of changing client preferences and account-based marketing will triumph.

As agencies adjust, evolve and recognise that technology and specialist skills can profoundly alter the existing relationship, undertaken by a situation analysis – they will be better informed as they invest and restructure to amplify one-to-one client engagements and marketing technology. However, before they do any of this, they should look inward and have an honest and frank discussion about their strengths and weaknesses to be in a stronger position to offer more specialist services and update their MarTech stacks.

Why are brands questioning the client-agency relationship and value proposition? The answer to this question could prove disastrous to agencies' bottom lines as brands consider the impact and value that their incumbent agency is providing. On the flipside, brands should also find the realistic nature of this shift and ask themselves if they are equipped to do the same job just as well, with limited resources? One thing for sure is that project-based work can be done relatively quickly and has the potential to increase revenue just as much as longer-term relationships. Agencies may look to hire independent digital transformation consultants to help them on their own transformation journey.

Agencies are historically good at researching and keeping up to date with industry trends but are they nimble enough to keep pace with the range of tactics that are required by their clients? The belief that brands need a more project-based solution will in itself transform the agency model over time. The allocation of client marketing managers for maintaining client control will continue to grow, and smaller more specialised projects may replace agency retainers. Agencies would benefit from stopping the promotion of all in one solution and instead focus on what they're good at and consolidate as opposed to bringing in the entire marketing and advertising scope of works. Ultimately brands and agencies need to work out how they can work better together.

Are consultants a valuable alternative option? Consultants can bring a fresh perspective to a fractured client-agency relationship. They have a deep understanding of the connective tissues between marketing/creative, business and digital/technology. As widespread disruption and competition increase with in-house projects, the practicalities of an outsider joining the relationship may be favourable for both sides of the coin as they may take on a mediation role. Working together to develop mutual understanding and help forge expert teams that can collaborate in new ways, may be worth the investment and efforts.

Consultants share an overarching objective to get the work done and thrive in new environments, in a way that can be both feasible and affordable. An agencies aim is to grow their clients' businesses and the sole driving force behind this partnership will be to deliver profitable, sustainable growth. Consultants can see things from both perspectives and advise on the best way to approach things.

Who are these new breeds of boutique agencies? Major global consultancies such as Deloitte, Accenture, IBM, KPMG, PwC, McKinsey and PricewaterhouseCoopers rank among the most aggressive players in the world and have all acquired agencies. Integrating branding, marketing, business and content expertise with core strategic offerings such as financial and technology services, data analytics and customer segmentation makes the consultancies attractive as an alternative partner. Consultancies know how to tap into a clients digital marketing budget and transform the business landscape through digital transformation projects-providing a blueprint for how consultancies and agencies can work together in the future and improve the client-agency relationship.

New Rules for Modern Marketers: Data Disruption & MarTech

Where once the role of a marketer was traditionally communication and campaign-focused the position is now disrupted by technology and compliance as they deal with a myriad of complexities of acquiring, understanding, translating, and leveraging data from an infinite amount of devices, platforms and channels. New challenges in data sensitivity and compliance surrounding GDPR, attribution modelling, cross-device identity, understanding technology landscape has reverberated marketers in a formidable way.

Research firm Forrester, predicts that spending on marketing automation technology will grow exponentially over the next few years', reaching $25 billion annually by 2030, an increase from $11.4 billion in 2017. Marketers are still in the early stages of adopting marketing automation technology.[3]

There is a growing need for Marketers to have real-time interactions (RTIM) and through-channel marketing automation (TCMA) platforms to become more agile and responsive. Marketers require the ability to automate tasks across multiple channels with campaign management software, lead-to-revenue management automation (L2RM), Content management platforms (CMP), cross-channel campaign management (CCCM) and marketing resource management (MRM) software. Marketing automation technology is predicted to double-digital growth as marketers reduce spend on other areas.[4] Forrester predicts partner relationship management (PRM) software market is to grow to $679 million by 2023, with a CAGR of 14.2 percent. PRM includes partner planning, recruitment, onboarding, enablement, incentives, co-selling, co-marketing, and management.[5] It is said that due to the growing volume and types of partners, managing a channel program is less of a linear approach and more on-demand with automated workflows, personalisation, customisation, and scalability.

How Can Marketers Leverage Data? Marketers need to make strategic decisions based on untapped data sources, ensuring datasets come together to inform each other in a responsible, ethical and sensitive way. Their role bleeds out into e-commerce and user experience, and they need to break down siloed databases from different departments. However, the consequence of this change is a more holistic customer journey generated through actionable insights and the agility to work with other functions – which will ultimately result in real-time measurable performance from their marcomms campaigns and advertising budgets. Data disruption and marketing technology have given marketers the power to understand user intent, create better value and build long-lasting relationships with their consumers.

As the wave of data disruption spreads through businesses around the world, new entrants with structural cost advantages and a "digital-first" business culture are setting new boundaries in a wide range of industries. These disruptors offer solutions that are often simpler, cheaper, or more convenient for customers. What do they all have in common? They leverage digital technologies, innovate rapidly to beat off the competition and understand that the customer leads the dance. Think Alibaba, Amazon & Netflix and how they have shifted the market faster than their competition. Nearly three quarters (72 percent) of more than 600 respondents to a survey say that their operations will be susceptible to this threat over the coming years.[6]

The rise in disruption means that consumers are expecting quality in their interactions with organisations, and their choices will be driven by how marketers deliver and meet those expectations. Marketers need to take creative steps to approach interactions, engagement and experiences with a personalised customer-obsessed mindset. As marketers are encouraged more and more towards the customer experience as a way to differentiate their company from their competitors and gain a clearer picture of their audiences- marketers need to grasp marketing technology to offer a CX that stands out from the crowd. They are required to tackle technology 'head-on' thus having the ability to navigate the increasingly cluttered

MarTech landscape to create, measure and report on outstanding innovative and data enriched campaigns.

Martech is the blending of marketing automation and technology solutions in various digital marketing channels. Martech helps marketers navigate the massive explosion and expanding array of marketing technologies available to them. Known as the 'Martech 5000' the 2018 Marketing Technology Landscape (Infographics 2018) lays out and organises 6,829 unique marketing technology solutions – that can help customer-centric marketers with their customer experience journey, learn more about visitors and how they interact with their brand. A Marketers martech stack is their secret weapon for marketing success – as they make use of technology, data, and leadership to drive bold digital transformation in their organisations and become fearless in their everyday activities.[7]

Martech is about people with the right skills making marketing platforms successful. A study from Moore Stephens and WARC reveals that brands in the UK and North America are expected to allocate somewhere around one-quarter of their budgets in 2018 to marketing technology. One in four respondents in the UK and Europe stated they have all the tools they need and fully utilise them. In the Asia-Pacific region, they are the most confident, with almost half (45%) feeling satisfied in their utilisation of marketing technology tools. More than two-thirds of marketers said they don't believe there's such a thing as the "perfect stack" for marketing technology, finding instead that it's always a work in progress which is unsurprising considering the landscape is evolving more rapidly than marketers can keep pace.[8]

Martech examples include: (Marketo/Hubspot/Salesforce) for CRM, (Hootsuite/Sprout Social) for social media, (Moz, Screaming Frog) for SEO, (MailChimp/Campaign Monitor) for email marketing platforms, (WordPress) for content management systems, (Google Trends/Keyword planner) for research tools, (Basecamp/Trello) for project management, (Slack/Asana) for comms, (Kissmetrics/Google Analytics) for analytics, and (SAP Cloud Platform) for machine learning, AI, blockchain, design thinking, data, analytics, IoT and data intelligence. All of which help marketers to efficiently and effectively execute innovative marketing activities. Depending on the size and needs of the business, martech stacks can come in different types, including many tools, across a large number of departments with the end goal of satisfying the changing needs of the customer.[9]

Virtually anyone involved with digital marketing is dealing with martech since digital by its very nature is technologically-based. The term "martech" especially applies to significant initiatives, efforts and tools that harness technology to achieve marketing goals and objectives. Changes in spending on media, martech and talent highlight the challenges of balancing short- and long-term needs. 22% of marketing budgets are allocated to marketing technologies. As marketing technology budgets exceed IT, they are indeed here to stay.[10]

Conclusion: The role of the modern marketer needs a stack of marketing and technology tools to deliver personalised, contextual content to customers in real-time to drive return-on-investment and improved customer experience. Technologies and techniques are changing exponentially that no individual alone can keep pace. While markers are required to understand the marketing technology landscape and become more data-driven to ensure a seamless and integrated customer journey, they certainly have their work cut out. Albeit being naturally inquisitive and intellectually curious, marketers will need to further their skill-set in an agile and rapidly expanding environment.

Chapter Six: AI & Machine Learning

Leveraging Data, AI and Machine Learning

Artificial Intelligence and Machine Learning are being implemented by decision-makers to allow marketers to tell stories at scale and better engage with their audience. Marketers are benefiting from gleaning valuable data insights to improve the speed, scale and effectiveness of their marketing campaigns to stay competitive and agile.

A research report reveals that just over half of marketers use AI, and an additional 27% are expected to incorporate AI technology in 2019. It's expected as the volume of consumer-generated data grows, AI computing techniques like machine learning, deep learning, and natural language processing (NLP) will become increasingly crucial to data-driven decision-making.[1] Key findings in the report by Business Insider explores the current and potential applications of AI within marketing:

- AI is advancing beyond data analysis and hurtling towards data generation as machines get better at automating sight and hearing. Insights gleaned from data-rich media such as voice and video is possible, and humans no longer have to categorise or describe various types of media manually.
- AI will transform marketers to become more efficient at planning and campaign execution in segmentation, tracking, and keyword tagging areas.
- 34% of global marketing executives chose AI, the

most of any option, when asked to choose which of the trending technology they felt most unprepared for.
- AI will help in content creation, but human marketers are still necessary. It's too soon for marketers to use AI to automatically create editorial content or select the right image and messaging for display ads. Machines will reduce production time, but humans are still needed for creativity.

How does AI present data to help marketers? AI exists to extract insights to make recommendations based on previously established criteria. It is a term used to describe a suite of unique, but related, technologies that include machine learning, deep learning, neural networks, natural language processing, and natural language generation (NLG). AI technology can process an enormous amount of unstructured data and decipher the natural language of that data which in turn can help marketers to optimise and personalise content. AI can be categorised in several ways including: Its capacity to mimic human characteristics.[2] The technologies powering AI systems are:

- Expert systems
- Machine learning
- Natural language processing
- Computer vision
- Automated speech recognition
- AI Planning

Conclusion: Companies that leverage analytics are creating customer value and outshining their competitors as they measure and build valuable insights to make informed business decisions. Companies that are implementing AI and machine learning technology is helping marketers to predict outcomes and devise strategies that capitalise on content performance and personalisation. It also aids content marketers in intelligently automating repetitive tasks to deliver the right message at the right time for the users intent. Using data insights enables marketers to optimise costs, sell more products and shape business priorities from a wealth of new information.

AI Marketing Analytics

Despite new technology trends offering digital marketers new and powerful capabilities, IT priorities are not aligned where customer-centricity and customer experience are concerned. Even though customers are in complete control of their journey from researching to consideration to decision making and eventually sharing experiences, marketing approaches still leave a lot to be desired. Connected savvy consumers expect personalised experiences, real-time engagement, relevance and simplicity.[3]

Mobile, real-time tech and social, has resulted in consumers being always on and as such are becoming more impatient because of on-demand apps, on-demand services and the influence of social media. However, new technology has arguably made marketers more risk-averse as they are sacrificing personalisation for marketing technology automation.[4]

Modern marketers need to adapt to personalisation, cross-channel and Omni-channel integration, responsive/adaptive design and dynamic customer engagement. Standards, mind-sets, checklists and legacy technologies are significant barriers to customer personalisation experience efforts. AI marketing analytics and machine learning, on the other hand, represents an enormous opportunity for marketers as it brings the capacity to extract useful insights from consumer data which can then be segmented and personalised intelligently. Consequently, the challenge is on the human front as marketers face unlearning everything they know by shifting from automation to personalisation-to anticipation and prediction.

AI marketing is more personal and human. The new era of AI marketing is where machines help marketing to become more personal and human by cutting out the guesswork. In turn, this frees up more time for marketers to understand customers thus allowing them to craft personalised messages, with relevant content on the device and channel they prefer and during times they wish to receive it. Marketers must be prepared to not only be more creative and data-driven, but they must also learn how customers are behaving and consider how AI can help disrupt what they know and how they measure success. Marketers should be open and possess curious minds to challenge conventions and assumptions to perform against evolving standards.[5]

Using the right data to get the correct answers allows for relevant engagement content and paths to deliver against maturing expectations and values. AI and machine learning converts data into insights and can offer a competitive advantage to those who can execute and measure its effects to react intelligently. The more the machine learns, the more it optimises new opportunities and understands friction points.

AI tools serve as a welcome addition to marketing stacks to drive a new marketing foundation for access to intelligent, automated and human-centred platforms for genuine, value-added consumer engagement. Intelligent AI involves the entire customer journey touchpoints and engagement strategies that enhance the customer experience throughout their journey and lifecycle. It is no longer about awareness, reach, and conversions. It focuses on growth, engagement and experiential metrics that go beyond vanity and tie into mutually beneficial outcomes.

Conclusion: The benefits of AI for an organisation can be enormous as automation on a large-scale will free up quality time for planning and allow leaders to focus on other creative areas that don't require repetitive tasks. AI and data are readily available to change the game, so marketers need to embrace and get smarter with their approach to analytics. AI marketing platforms convert customer data and activities into actionable, personalised insights, which leads to more relevant and personalised cross-channel consumer engagement.

Chapter Seven: Digital Strategies

Business Value of APIs

Businesses are discovering valuable new ways to engage and connect with its customers and to create new business opportunities and improve existing products, systems, and operations with application programming interfaces (APIs). Consumers are connecting with businesses through the web, mobile, and social apps. By developing private and public APIs, companies can offer their employees and partners new tools to put data to use that will help them streamline operations and serve customers better.

APIs are driving innovation, and the need for businesses to develop and execute successful API strategies in a dynamic environment is strengthening and fueling the API economy. A useful API can give existing and potential customers new reasons to interact and connect with a business on more of a personal level as they share their experiences with others.[1] APIs are no longer just another piece of technology — they make digital society and digital business work.

APIs form the touchpoints between platforms and ecosystems and have the ability to open up new business channels, new partner integrations and new markets. In some cases, APIs can be in response to a particular industry and CIOs are turning to APIs as enablers of digital transformations to start a platform business on which to build an ecosystem as part of their digital strategy.[2]

Digital platforms underpin the creation of new business models by integrating ecosystems of people, business and things.[3] Publishing APIs is top of mind for savvy companies looking to gain strides in the API economy, as they begin to experiment with the delivery of APIs and explore how the platform will work in collaboration with partners within the ecosystem. Running an API program is not the only way to build a platform and an ecosystem, but it's a good start for some organisations. However, without full lifecycle API management, it is impossible to run an effective program.

"APIs are most valuable for creating new business models and streamlining selling strategies across all channels. The greatest revenue potential they provide is removing barriers to growing revenue by integrating platforms and apps so organizations can quickly launch new business models and scale fast".[4]

Managing application programming interfaces throughout their lifecycle is becoming more prevalent as platforms and ecosystems grow due to the demands of digital transformation and use of APIs in our everyday lives. The developers' role is to target, market to and govern communities of developers who embed the APIs through a portal.

With full lifecycle management and the advent of the API economy, consumers are now often outside of the organisation and endpoint protection. Whereas in the past, APIs were primarily developed and consumed within a single organisation and development group. This was to ensure that APIs met the needs of their consumers through a shared understanding of the domain and the functionality. API management buying centres will continue to shift from traditional IT departments to business units or single government agencies.

As businesses add newer software and services and modern APIs to existing systems to solve their organisational challenges, they may come across problems with custom point-to-point integrations, this is because legacy systems often are not interoperable with newer technologies.[5] Another challenge is the lack of access and resources to useful tools for designing, testing, and monitoring, along with a developer community. When a business wants to develop their API strategy, they should look for feedback and insights into the user design and features from the community before being widely adopted to ensure that an API is engaging and well-crafted.

The basic principle of the economy is that APIs can be new products to open up new business channels that a company can offer, or to sell more of its traditional products. There are several business models associated with the publishing of APIs and companies gain different types of value from publishing APIs or running hackathons. The most common model is an indirect one, whereby a company provides free access to its APIs. Companies might do this in return for a quicker, more efficient execution of a business process, such as the ordering of goods in a supply chain. Alternatively, they might do so to increase sales of a traditional product.[6]

Conclusion: Smartphone apps are part of our daily lives and as we check our emails, share photos on social apps we are using APIs. Every time we click a link to find information, buy or reserve something, we are using APIs. Moreover, each time a digital business platform connects with partners or new affiliates, it is using APIs. They support self-service and a one-to-many relationship between provider and consumers and are present in every part of our digital world and into the very fabric of a digital business. A full lifecycle API management platform is needed to build ecosystems and run an effective program. APIs will increase exponentially in the future as already hundreds are published every month, and thousands are tested by developers every day. Understanding which APIs to offer to which developers, internal or external, can be challenging, as can the task of securing the necessary corporate data. APIs will most certainly continue to fuel the API economy as will the need for quick execution that focuses on fewer applications at any one time.

Chapter Eight: Digital Transformation

Disruption of Enterprise Architecture

Organisations of all shapes and sizes across the globe are embarking on digital transformation (DX) a term that is synonymous with undertaken an overhaul of traditional processes with the adaption of a digital-front-end. In reality, digital transformation is about adapting business culture and methods to work with new technology. There are many challenges a business will go through during this transition period, below are some challenges organisations face that fuel digital transformation programs:

Operational silos: Functional and data silos already exist because many companies organise themselves around products or channels, not the customer.

Existing systems: Systems of records and channel-specific technologies, often with their own rules and logic, and little ability to talk to each other, resulting in fragmented customer journeys.

Cultural change: Various departments have different objectives and key performance indicators which can sometimes undermine the collaboration and cultural change.

Understanding Data: Need to analyse data to uncover valuable insights about customers to be applied to both historical and real-time contextual data.

In today's fast-moving digital era, customers expect accurate and timely responses and decisions, regardless of the channel through which they engage with a brand. Using data-driven insights to understand customer behaviour can feed into business strategy and decision-making. It involves businesses to make use of both structured and unstructured data, pulling together data from many sides of the company to help drive the transformation journey and respond quickly to any change or event that may occur. Innovations in technology, storage, analytics and visualisation all provide a digital landscape that can turn data insights into a meaningful business context that help an organisation to be much better informed. The biggest challenge is to create real, sustainable value from Insights & Data that goes far beyond any proof-of-concept or pilot installation.[1]

Data Analytics

Data and analytics capabilities has progressed in recent years and the volume of available data has grown exponentially as more sophisticated algorithms have been developed, and computational power and storage steadily improved. The convergence of data trends is fueling rapid technology advances and business disruptions. However, most companies are capturing only a tiny amount of the potential value from data and analytics. Progress has occurred in location-based services and in retail and new opportunities have arisen making the gap between the leaders and laggards even larger. Barriers that companies face in extracting value from data and analytics are regarded as organisational; as many struggle to incorporate data-driven insights into the day-to-day business processes. Challenges also include attracting and retaining the right talent and capabilities. Data driven companies are using their capabilities to improve their core operations. Network effects of digital platforms are creating wins in dynamic markets. Data is now seen as a critical corporate asset. Data and analytics underpin several disruptive models and by introducing new types of datasets we are seeing industries disrupting, and data integration capabilities breaking through organisational and technological silos, enabling new insights and models. Data and analytics above all, enables faster and more evidence based decision making.

Conclusion: Data and analytics are transforming multiple industries, and the effects will continue to become apparent as adoption reaches critical mass. As deep learning reaches maturity, enabling machines unprecedented capabilities to think, problem-solve and understand language organisations that harness such capabilities effectively will be able to create significant value and differentiate, while others find themselves at a disadvantage.[2]

Digital business transformation objectives & strategies

Digital business transformation objectives is a hot topic for business leaders which is unsurprising when we consider the growth of DX spending and future predictions worldwide. Regarding strategy, there is no doubt advice is abundant as experts and consultants are vying for the attention of CXOs on which approaches they should take. Like anything in digital business, setting business goals and objectives from an initial strategy requires a clear roadmap to execute and deliver outcomes. A suitable transformation journey will include all the necessary steps and approaches so that once the transformation objectives are selected, there's a framework for IT and new innovative ways of working in an agile environment.

As aforementioned, there are many reasons companies embark on a transformational journey, and each organisation will have a different set of transformation objectives with varying priorities, be it to improve business processes and reduce costs, differentiate products/services in the marketplace, gain competitive advantage, optimise and simplify infrastructure, understand insights from data analytics to make better decisions or the need to redesign business models and rethink operations to improve agility, cost-effectiveness and flexibility. Other reasons may include adopting new ways of working to increase productivity, retention, loyalty and enhance the digital customer experience. The goal of any transformation should be a sustainable step change in organisational performance and health.³

Examples of digital business transformation objectives:

- Adopt new ways of working to become more fluid and accelerate workflows;
- Understand opportunities and threats in industry disruption;
- Analyse digital products/services and operational performance;
- Adoption of technology, cloud-based apps, people analytics;
- Promote project-team approaches, ensuring customer data is accessible;
- Define new roles and develop new skills and capabilities in data analytics;
- Develop a Chief Digital Officer role and appoint sponsors for each business unit;
- Analyse value chain, customer touchpoints and improve the customer experience;
- Considerations for creating a centre of excellence (COE) for project management and leadership.

For strategy development, architectural frameworks, and practical execution there are fundamental approaches that are shaping how IT services are produced and consumed; agile, DevOps, software-as-a-service infrastructure, intelligent automation, personas and context, and finally, digital service management.⁴ Regarding practical execution, business managers can select from options based on their specific needs. For example, for the digital customer experience, we need a new set of capabilities including a persona-driven approach, omnichannel integration, customer centricity, and insights from analytics. Another key enabler is 'advanced cybersecurity' due to emerging technologies that are not entirely secure from the start. Organisation may struggle to implement various security controls which leads to delays in realising their full business benefits.

The core SMAC stack is evolving with the rise of mobility in wearable technologies and the cloud is evolving and embracing broader concepts such as hybrid IT and software-defined data centres. These key disruptive technologies now serve as the foundational building blocks in the new digital business platform ecosystem of on-demand services. Taking a holistic view across all these enablers can help to maximise business benefits and unlock new forms of value in the years ahead.

The aforementioned approaches that are shaping how IT services are produced and consumed are accelerating digital service development and deployment. In turn, making services accessible and on-demand, automate extensively, personalise to specific roles, and manage holistically. Progress in these areas will help an organisation master the digital services lifecycle concerning digital touch points, interactions and transactions with customers.

Conclusion: Digital business transformation objectives will endeavour to focus on technology as an essential factor to consider as IT continues to be a hybrid environment. An agile and iterative journey to the 'future platform' can simultaneously optimise infrastructure and simplify management on the back end (the IT transformation), as well as improve the user experience and transform business processes on the front end (the business transformation). A business can gain an early advantage for customers and end users at the same time as IT transforms its delivery model. Finally, regarding change management, CIOs/CMOs and business leaders don't have to create entirely new processes or reinvent the wheel, to execute on digital initiatives. Existing corporate funding opportunities and corporate innovation mechanisms can be fine-tuned to enhance business models and objectively transform into a digital business.

Transformation Challenges Facing Leaders

Digital business transformation is a common theme in organisations today. The accelerated pace at which digital innovation is disrupting industries is impelling CEOs and leaders to take action. Digital transformation programs exist to change how a company engages with its people, processes and technology along with the development of infrastructure and capability alignment to meet business goals. The reasons to drive transformations are broad in scope and impact as they are carried out in conjunction with ongoing operations.

According to the Project Management Institute, (PMI), Transformation programs require a tailored approach to applications of a standard project and program management to meet the unique challenges regarded with managing people as well as building leadership and ownership among key program stakeholders. Critical success factors for programs are the overall transformation approach to the management of processes and structures.[5]

As organisations embrace digital business transformations, they focus not only on delivering enterprise-wide IT capabilities that complement business priorities, but also on their employees to address talent acquisition, retention and churn on productivity, as well as quality, service and employee engagement programs. CEOs want to increase performance and develop new capabilities that the organisation did not previously have and transformations start by a sense of urgency and a compelling case for action that will result in a significant impact on functions within the organisation.

The "Digital" in Business Transformation

Harvard Business Review defines 'Business Transformation' as making fundamental changes in how business is conducted to cope with shifts in the market environment. Business Transformation has three key elements: Digital, Enterprise and IT Functionality and Technology which primarily focuses on newer, cutting-edge technical capability adopted in an enterprise.

THE RISE OF DIGITAL DISRUPTION

Different aspects of transformation programs include:

1. Business transformation – encompasses the cultural shift and business processes driven by changing market demands; i.e., the company's culture of change and business drivers.
2. Digital transformation - encompasses the tools and processes implemented to support business transformation; i.e., applications.
3. IT transformation - the reassessment and overhaul of information technology to support digital transformation; i.e., infrastructure.[6]

MIT Sloan Management Review, interviewed 157 executives in 50 different companies to find out how they were moving forward with digital transformation at varying paces and at what varying levels of success. They found that none of the companies they interviewed is transforming all areas at once and suggests that leading "digital" change requires managers to have a vision of how to transform their company into a digital world.[7]

Nine elements of digital transformation:

1. Customer Understanding - Companies are starting to take advantage of previous investments in legacy systems to understand specific geographies and market segments.
2. Top Line Growth - Companies are using technology to enhance sales conversations. Financial services companies, for example, are using tablet-based presentations instead of paper-based slide decks to make sales pitches.
3. Customer Touch Points - Customer service is being enhanced significantly by digital initiatives. As an example a bank established a Twitter account to answer client complaints quickly, helping customers avoid going physically to a branch.

4. Process Digitisation - Automation enables companies to refocus their people on more strategic tasks. A manufacturer has begun to centralise the HR function, allowing economies of scale through self-service allowing HR people to focus on management skills, rather than counting days off.
5. Worker Enablement - Individual-level work has, in essence, been virtualized separating the work process from the location of the work.
6. Performance Management - Transactional systems give executives more profound insights into products, regions and customers, which allows for decisions to be made on real data, not on assumptions.
7. Digitally Modified Businesses - Finding ways to augment physical with digital offerings and to use digital to share content across organisational silos and building digital or service wrappers around traditional products.
8. New Digital Businesses - Companies are introducing digital products that complement traditional products.
9. Digital Globalization - Companies are increasingly transforming from multinational to global operations.

I-Scoop, argues that digital transformation encompasses all aspects of business, regardless of whether it concerns a digital business or not. In times when the acceleration of technology adoption and change leads to an entirely new market, customer and business (people, capabilities, processes, models) realities, opportunities and challenges, ultimately lead to a new economy- what IDC calls the DX economy.[8]

As consumers expect a conscious seamless customer experience, digital technology is affecting company's in different ways as they embrace design thinking and how best to restructure policies and practices to keep pace with the forever changing digital and business landscape. A Harvard Business Review article titled "To Lead a Digital Transformation, CEOs Must Prioritize" states that "becoming a digital leader is not simply a matter of technological savvy. It's about creating an agile organisation that can detect what type of change is essential and respond quickly to the most competitive solution".[9]

Business leaders of tomorrow need a holistic view of the digital threats and opportunities facing critical parts of the business and understand how to link them to an overall vision for how digital is reshaping the competitive landscape.

Considerations for Digital Business Transformation

Digital Transformation programs encompass change management in business processes, technology adoption, application deployments, infrastructure consolidation and talent management. Plans involve multiple initiatives that require prioritisation, sequencing and coordination to deliver results from a clear vision of benefits. CEOs may have already decided to launch their app, deployed artificial Intelligence, machine learning and robotics, or maybe already taking advantage of data analytics to make better decisions as pressures of a competitive marketplace and shifting technologies circles the C-suite. However, it is essential that efforts coordinate, and a framework be implemented to ensure the best initiatives don't fail to get the attention and investment they need.[10]

Conclusion: As digital business transformation technologies and investments continue to grow, the pressure is on to transform workplaces and find innovative ways to engage with their customers. CEOs are needing to understand which technologies they should invest in, and prioritise change management activities around the business operations, people and customers. As digital technology moves faster than some budgets allow and the choices are endless, CEOs will need to keep pace, empower people and set a clear vision for business transformation. Visualisation tools, customer data, analytics, knowledge sharing, project-based assignments are some vital consideration for cultural change and digital business transformation success.[11]

Worldwide Digital Transformation Predictions

Spending on worldwide Digital Transformation will be $2 trillion in 2022 as Organisations Commit to DX. Spending is expected to steadily expand upto 2022 achieving a five-year compound annual growth rate of 16.7%.[12] There will be four industries responsible for nearly half of the $1.25 trillion in 2019 which is said to be discrete manufacturing to the value of ($220 billion), process manufacturing to the value of ($135 billion), transportation to the value of ($116 billion), and finally, retail to the value of ($98 billion). For discrete and process manufacturing industries, the highest DX spending priority is said to be smart manufacturing. The IDC expects both industries to invest more than $167 billion in smart manufacturing as well as significant investments in digital innovation ($46 billion), and digital supply chain ($29 billion). The transportation industries leading strategic priority is digital supply chain optimisation, which is to the value of approximately $65 billion in spending. For the retail industry, the top priority is omni-channel commerce, which will drive investments of more than $27 billion including omni-channel commerce platforms, augmented virtual experience, in-store contextualised marketing, and next-generation payments.

Predictions from IDC FutureScape relating to Worldwide Digital Transformations are:

Prediction 1: By 2020, at least 55% of organisations will be digitally determined, and markets will transform and reimagine the future through new business models and digital products and services.

Prediction 2: By 2022, the CDO title will erode, as digital will have become fully embedded, however, more than 60% of CEOs will have spent part of their careers leading digital initiatives.

Prediction 3: By 2020, Customer advocacy will result in 60% of

B2C brands embracing net promoter score as their leading success metric.

Prediction 4: By 2020, 80% of enterprises will enhance enterprise functions, strengthening competitiveness, and creating new sources of revenue and create data management and monetization capabilities.

Prediction 5: By 2020, 30% of G2000 companies will have implemented advanced digital twins of their operational processes, which will enable flatter organizations and one-third fewer knowledge workers.

Prediction 6: By 2023, 35% of workers will start working with bots or other forms of AI, requiring company leaders to redesign operational processes, performance metrics, and recruitment strategies.

Prediction 7: By 2020, 30% of G2000 companies will have allocated capital budget equal to at least 10% of revenue to fuel their digital strategies.

Prediction 8: By 2021, prominent in-industry value chains, enabled by blockchains, will have extended their digital platforms to their entire omni-experience ecosystems, thus reducing transaction costs by 35%.

Prediction 9: By 2021, about 30% of manufacturers and retailers globally will have built digital trust through blockchain services that enable collaborative supply chains and allow consumers to access product histories.

Prediction 10: By 2023, 95% of entities will have incorporated new digital KPI sets — focusing on product/service innovation rates, data capitalization, and employee experience — to navigate the digital economy.

With direct digital transformation investment spending of $5.5 trillion over the years 2018 to 2021, (DX) spending will continue to be a central area of business leadership thinking," said Shawn Fitzgerald, research director, Worldwide Digital Transformation Strategies. The IDC's 2019 DX predictions represent our perspective on the major transformation trends over the next five years. With almost 800 business use cases spanning 16 industries and eight functional areas, this DX spending illustrates where industry is both prioritising digital investments and where the largest growth in 3rd Platform and innovation accelerator technologies.[13]

Sana, an integrated e-commerce solution for Microsoft Dynamics and SAP, commissioned Sapio Research to survey over 300 automotive, food and beverage, construction and electronics companies worldwide to pinpoint the main trends in B2B e-commerce and digital transformation. The report found that key UK figures showed 86% respondents said the ease of online purchase was the main reason for wanting online access. 52% say that being unable to connect sales channels was a hurdle in implementing a digital transformation project. A Further 11% said it was about the journey and not the destination.

Other key goals examined included reducing the cost of sale, improving the customer experience, and supporting sales staff. 95% of businesses revealed that they were planning to undergo digital transformation compared to only 5% stating that they weren't planning on doing the same. 56% of respondents believe that customer demands are the reason to optimise their IT infrastructure and 70% was due to competitive pressure. Interestingly, while 28% said that reviewing the security of the IT infrastructure is a severe challenge, 15% state that the primary challenge is caused by unrealistic goals and return on investment.[14]

Conclusion: Worldwide Digital Transformation is affecting every industry as enterprise transformations take place for the benefit of becoming more digitally capable. Competition in the market and demand from customers is verifying the need to transition to a digital-native organisation. Laggards will suffer the consequences of being left behind while other industries are forgoing a transitioning period. The IT industry will face industry disruption through multiplied innovations. Organisations that embrace change by leveraging new tools and a digital business strategy will be at the heart of successful digital transformation.

Chapter Nine: Emerging Technologies

Human Machine Partnerships

Emerging technologies continue to have a significant impact on the remodelling of businesses and culture in recent times. The rate at which machines and humans are working together in tandem is propelling at rapid speed. The rise of sophisticated technology advancements such as Artificial Intelligence, Augmented and Virtual Reality, Robotics, and Cloud Computing, are driving many academics, entrepreneurs, and enterprises to envision a transformative future for a digital society. These advances in software will underpin developments in science, engineering, technology and communications. New jobs will be reimagined as automation replaces human labour. Companies are aware of the benefits of cloud technology regarding efficiency, agility and profitability.

In a research study of 4,000 senior decision makers, 45 % say they are concerned that in 3-5 years their jobs will become obsolete and nearly half don't know what their industry will look like by this time. Furthermore, 73% believe they need to be more 'digital' to succeed in the future.[1] The report explains that due to the commercial success and adoption of robots in manufacturing, we will see them expand into the workplace and homes with the likes of caregiving and civic robots. As deep learning improves robots' abilities to empathise and reason they will become commonplace. However, there are still cultural acceptance hurdles, legal and regulatory concerns to overcome until they are fully integrated into our personal lives. It is suggested that human-machine partnerships will enhance daily activities around the coordination of resources as well as in-the-moment learning, which will change expectations for work-requiring corporate structures to adapt and learn to the expanding capabilities of human-machine teams.

Digital technologies will integrate with machine learning to create a population of digital orchestration systems, and by 2030, digital conductors will be a highly sought-after skill set. Humans will need to strengthen their ability to team up with machines to produce optimal outcomes. Human-machine partnerships will help automate and coordinate people's lives, but they will also transform how organisations find talent, manage teams, deliver products and services, and support professional development. Human-machine partnerships will, therefore, change and reset the working landscape and the tasks and duties of the jobs they'll perform.

Conclusion: The incredible capabilities of today's emerging technologies will fuel human-machine collaboration and codependence to create a future where people partner with machines to build respective strengths and improve lives at home and in the workplace.

Emerging Technology Trends

Gartner states that emerging trends in 2019 and beyond are blockchain, quantum computing, augmented analytics, artificial intelligence that will drive disruption and create new business models.[2] The future will be characterised by smart devices that deliver increasingly insightful digital services everywhere, with what Gartner describes as being "intelligent digital mesh".

Intelligent: How AI exists in every technology, creating entirely new categories.

Digital: The blending of digital and physical worlds to create an immersive world.

Mesh: Exploiting connections between sets of people, businesses, devices, content and services.

EMERGING TECHNOLOGIES

Furthermore, trends under these three themes are seen as a key ingredient in driving a continuous innovation process. Gartner's Top 10 Strategic Technology trends highlight changes or not yet widely recognised trends that will impact and transform industries through 2023.

1. Autonomous Things

All autonomous things use AI to interact naturally with their environments such as cars or robots. They exist across five categories and are as follows:

Robotics;
Vehicles;
Drones;
Appliances;
Agents.

They occupy four environments including: Sea, land, air and digital and operate with different degrees of capability, coordination and also intelligence.

2. Augmented Analytics

We have increasing amounts of data from which to draw conclusions and explore all possibilities. Augmented analytics is said to represent a third major wave for data and analytics capabilities. Data science and machine learning platforms are transforming how a business generates analytical insights. Gartner says by 2020, 40% of data science tasks will be automated, resulting in increased productivity and broader use by citizen data scientists.

3. AI-driven Development

AI-driven development refers to tools, technologies and best practices for embedding AI into applications and the use of AI to create

AI- tools for development. There will be a market shift from a focus on data scientists currently partnered with developers to that of developers operating independently. This allows more developers to utilise the services, and increases efficiency which leads to more mainstream usage of virtual software developers and non-professionals.

4. Digital Twins

Digital twins refers to the digital representation of a real-life object, process or a system. They can be linked to create twins of larger systems, such as a power plant or a city. Today's digital twins support specific business outcomes, that link to the real world, potentially in real time for monitoring and control used in the application of advanced big data analytics and AI. Digital twins of an organisation are emerging to create models of organisational process to enable real time monitoring and drive improved process efficiencies.

5. Empowered Edge

Edge computing is information processing and content collection and delivery that are placed closer to the sources of the information. This technology is a result for IoT systems to deliver disconnected or distributed capabilities into the world of IoT. Here technology and thinking will shift to the point at which people are connected through hundreds of these edge devices. Gartner expects by 2028, an increase in the embedding of sensors, storage computers and advanced AI capabilities in edge devices and general intelligence will shift toward the edge, in endpoint devices, such as industrial devices, screens, smartphones and automobile power generators.

6. Immersive Technologies

Through 2028, conversational platforms and technologies like augmented reality (AR), mixed reality (MR) and virtual reality (VR), will change how users perceive the world, and lead to a new immersive experience. AR, MR and VR are said to enable improved productivity, and the next generation of VR will be able to sense shapes and track a user's position. MR will enable people to view, and interact with their world differently. By 2022, 70% of enterprises globally will be experimenting with immersive technologies for improved consumer experiences and enterprise use, with 25% deploying them into production.

The future of conversational platforms, ranging from virtual personal assistants to chatbots, will incorporate sensory channels that enable the platform to detect emotions based on facial expressions, as they become more conversational during interactions.

7. Digital Ethics and Privacy

Consumers now understand the value of their personal information, and are increasingly concerned with how their data is used by public and private companies. Companies are at risk of consumer backlash if they don't pay attention and conversations regarding privacy must strive toward ethics and trust. Governments are planning or passing more regulations for companies to be compliant, and consumers are being more careful about information available about themselves. Companies must gain and maintain trust at all times.

8. Quantum Computing

Quantum computing -a type of nonclassical computing represents information as elements denoted as quantum bits or "qubits."

Quantum computers are highly scalable and highly parallel computing models. They are able to theoretically work on millions of computations at any one time. Commercially they are an available, affordable and reliable service that would transform some industries. This technology is in an emerging state, meaning it is an opportune time for businesses to consider them and understand the potential applications and security implications.

9. Blockchain

Blockchain, is a type of cryptographically signed, irrevocable transactional records that are shared by all participants in the network. Blockchain enables companies to trace transactions and work with untrusted parties without the need of a bank. This reduces business friction and currently finance, government, healthcare, manufacturing, supply chain and other industries are using this technology. Blockchain could potentially lower costs, reduce transactions and businesses should evaluate the need for this technology, as it is estimated that blockchain will create $3.1T in business value by 2030.

10. Smart Spaces

Smart spaces are physical or digital environments in which humans and technology-enabled systems interact in open and connected ecosystems. AI-driven technology, together with edge computing, blockchain and digital twins are driving toward this trend as individual solutions become smart spaces. Smart spaces are evolving to include five dimensions: openness, connectedness, coordination, intelligence and scope. Smart spaces as individual technologies are emerging from silos to work together to create a collaborative and interaction environment. An example of smart spaces is smart cities, where areas combine business, residential and industrial communities that have been designed using intelligent urban ecosystem frameworks for linking social and community collaboration.

Chapter Ten: Customer Experience

Innovation & Customer Touchpoints

As CMOs fine-tune the customer experience at every touch point within the customer journey, focus is on digital transformation and the selection of cutting-edge technology to improve the customer experience. Leading enterprise software provider SAP brings new technologies and services together to help businesses power their digital transformation.

The SAP Leonardo platform, aids in design thinking services and expertise to help fast-track digital transformation. It allows businesses to use the system to adopt new business models and capabilities rapidly – and add future technologies as they emerge – essential ingredients to digital business success, innovation and becoming a data-driven business.[1]

Understanding the benefits of customer experience is crucial for companies to stay ahead of the competition. Company culture is a critical success factor in digital transformation initiatives. SAP's recent Digital Transformation Executive Study finds 70% of leaders have seen significant or transformational value from the digital transformation in customer satisfaction and engagement. While 92% of leaders report that they already have mature digital transformation strategies and processes in place to improve the overall customer experience versus just 22% for all others.[2]

Customer needs, roles and responsibilities pave the way to advancing customer transformation in several ways:

- Own customer journeys
- Implement improvement measures
- Catalyse performance improvement
- Overcome organisational barriers
- Understand each touchpoint within a context
- Identify universal pain points and develop solutions

The complexity of customer journeys, in which a customer can leap from touchpoint to touchpoint across channels, highlights the need for cross-functional collaboration and adapting operations to enhance customer experience.[3] With more than 500 executives and digital strategists were surveyed to understand their current challenges and opportunities as they undergo a digital transformation. The results reveal that "evolving customer behaviours and preferences is a top driver of digital transformation, fewer than half (28%) invest in understanding digital customers. Chief Information Officer's (CIOs) is most often at the helm.[4] As all companies increasingly become "technology companies," the roles of the CIO and IT department are more critical than ever — but real success in digital transformation is an enterprise-wide, cross-functional endeavour. The employee experience is a crucial, yet often overlooked element of a successful digital transformation. Companies and their change agents still face significant challenges in the pursuit of digital transformation with 31% of executives, and digital strategists say that digital transformation is a cost centre and not an investment. With 31.4% Saying it is because a lack of digital talent and expertise and 31% putting it down to general cultural issues.

Conclusion: Digital transformation processes are led by customer experience. Therefore resulting in digital transformation ranking high on the agenda of many organisations striving towards a more customer-centric view around experiences, strategic decisions surrounding the overall customer journey and technology adoption.The employee experience is also crucial, yet often an overlooked element of digital transformation.

Chapter Eleven: Workforce Evolution

Culture, HR Tools & Remote Working

With the rise of globalisation, remote and flexible working, the teamwork landscape is changing as we know it, resulting in a global workforce evolution. HR functions are transforming with HR technology, talent management and organisational culture. Chief Human Resource Officers' (CHROs) or Chief People Officers' (CPOs), now need to contend with providing resources as they evolve with rapidly changing expectations to ensure talent people strategies reflect the skills and employment structures of the future. Decision-making regarding technology capabilities, market trends, employee experience and data influences company growth.

The HR environment is evolving due to employees taking more control of their employment experience, forcing companies to assume the role that culture plays within their organisation seriously. Getting culture right increases higher employee performance and overall better engagement. According to McKinsey, The ten most basic issues facing leaders are: attracting and retaining talent, developing talent, managing performance, creating leadership teams, making decisions, reorganising to capture value quickly, reducing overhead costs for the long term, making culture a competitive advantage, leading transformational change, and transitioning to new leadership roles.[1] "Digital and consumer marketing are permeating new ways of recruiting, working, learning, and engaging employees. Applying a consumer and digital lens is much more than just incorporating new solutions in HR. Being employee-centered and digital-first is about having a new mindset, plus a set of consumer-focused and technological skills to creating new HR solutions."[2]

As a new culture of work takes shape, senior HR officers' are striving toward creating high-performing teams where coherence around goals, ideas, actions, and values are efficient and innovative. New HR technology, generation communication preferences and project-led collaboration and teamwork are bringing new expectations and norms such as remote and freelance working. In today's competitive environment, sharing information and expertise can be critical in driving both individual and organisational success. Such forces are driven by forward-thinking business leaders and younger workers who have grown up in digital and can work collaboratively. HR technology is fuelling teamwork disruption and given rise to employee engagement platforms to build meaningful integrations between HR to enhance a company strategies. HR should be willing to understand the technology available and follow trends and take data-driven risks.[3]

Microsoft asked 14,000 people from seven countries in various stages of their career how they collaborate at work and found that regardless of generation, 61% of respondents prefer short communication as opposed to long and detailed forms. Furthermore, generations view technology differently. With 79% stating that using the newest technology made them more satisfied and 61 % saying that they felt like their workplace was behind the times when it comes to keeping up with the latest communication technology trends.[4]

Unsurprisingly, remote workers value collaboration technology twice as much as non-remote workers. Adding to that is 42% of U.S. workers currently spending 60% of their time working remotely. Astonishingly, the majority of U.S. workers are predicted to be in a freelance capacity by 2027 according to 'Freelancing in America: 2017' a study commissioned by Freelancers Union and Upwork. Findings also revealed that freelancers are better prepared for the future and are increasingly freelancing by choice as stability is redefined.

Chief Information Officers', are looking at how they can create a single, shared workspace for conversations, media and tools which empower engagement and knowledge sharing through community apps and social tools. People analytics data are helping HR professionals to understand where productivity can work smarter. Enterprises will need to change in order to help people develop more rapidly and achieve ever higher levels of performance. People and performance are foundational to the postdigital enterprise. Once you accept people, you will start to see the importance of a third "p" for "places" in which people need to perform their work, which for most businesses has become a blend of virtual and physical environments.[5] Feedback, engagement, & analytics tools reign and there is a massive shift from automation to productivity, 2018 will see the full emergence of the integrated engagement platform, which will combine features and benefits from closely related technology categories, such as well-being, recognition, learning, and engagement measurement.[6]

Culture is embedded in the very fabric of every company and defined as the underlying norms, values and beliefs that drive employee behaviour. It is arguably the single most crucial factor in an organisation's success or failure. Senior partner of Hay Group's Leadership Development Practice states in a "Real World Leadership" study "Culture is no longer seen as an afterthought when considering the business focus of an organisation. Culture is the X-factor. It's the invisible glue that holds an organisation together and ultimately makes the difference between whether an organisation can succeed in the market or not." The comprehensive global study of 7,500 executives from 107 different countries found that "driving culture change" is among the top three priorities for global leadership development. Culture runs through every touchpoint and should be aligned with business goals so that employees follow suit to improve organisational performance. 72% of respondents agreed that culture is vital to corporate performance. However, only 32% said their culture aligns with their business strategy. Culture should support employees from different generations and offer a diverse and collaborative workforce strategy for long-term goals and desires of both remote and non-remote workers.[7]

HR technology is enhancing collaboration and enabling innovation in the workplace. As remote and freelance work continues to increase, so too will video-based collaboration tools. Workforce flexibility will have its advantages but also challenges as CPOs ensure employees feel supported with the right types of benefits to that of their counterparts. HR will need to think beyond the traditional full-time employee and work environment by putting processes in place to help remote employees feel connected, challenged and empowered.[8]

Conclusion: The time has come for HR to concentrate on creating a more personalised approach with the aid of technology and data to shape workforce strategy, drive employee engagement and contribute directly to business performance. Organisations must transform their structures, processes, and cultures to create trust and openness. Companies that put people at the heart of their business will thrive.

Unlocking the Benefits of HR Technology Investment

Chief Human Resource Officers, are seeking HR technology investment as they consider innovative ways and cutting-edge technologies and tools to remain competitive and drive the right talent decisions for attracting and retaining top talent – a critical strategy for change management and digital transformation success. However, HR professionals may be feeling the pressure to present a business case for investments, upgrades and workplace tools adoption and may struggle to confidently communicate the challenges and unlock the benefits of shifting toward teams and productivity tools.[9]

As workforce tools are being approved and implemented and people analytics analysed, CEOs want to know what benefits new HR technology will have on the overall business. According to HR Technologist "The key to convincing top management lies not merely in knowing your HR facts and figures, but also in garnering the necessary pan-organisation support, by highlighting the current and future takeaways." As HR leaders seek technology investment, the need to communicate the benefits and reasons for wanting to use technology is essential to gaining sponsorship from key stakeholders.[10] More than ever, employers want their core systems and platforms to integrate seamlessly with their data to give them better insights into their workforce. Thus now we're seeing a massive wave of upgrades and a surge in more HR technology than ever with "cloud-based technologies and new infrastructures of team-oriented, app- and data-centric, network-based applications for HR".[11]

The growing use of apps, big data, real-time communication, and increasing use of artificial intelligence (AI), cognitive bots, virtual reality (VR) and intelligent predictive software are the main reasons why the HR technology landscape is changing. Also, changes in the way we work and manage teams are also affecting the market as companies want to make work life more comfortable and more productive for their employees. Companies are operating as networks of groups meaning they require HR technology and organisational network analysis (ONA), and tools to assist in this hyperactive new working environment which is resulting in a rise of team-centric tools, platforms, coaching, analytics, monitoring and assessment tools.[12]

Conclusion: The future of work is changing rapidly as employers of all sizes experience digital transformation. Careful consideration of which HR technology investments to make internally for empowering the workforce is enabling Human Resource Transformation. The driving force behind employers switching their HR technology is down to changes in the overall technology landscape, changes in the way we work, and changes in the way we manage organisations, information and people. Companies must deploy talent in new ways to remain competitive as the future of work and organisations become more fluid. An integrated system removes inefficiencies, empowering the workforce and making each employee feel valued. Business strategy is no longer about planning ahead but instead about sensing and seizing new opportunities and adapting to a continually changing complex environments with networks of teams at the helm.

Chapter Twelve: Fourth Industrial Revolution

Industry 4.0

Civilisation is on the verge of the next industrial revolution coined 'Industry 4.0'. A term used to refer to the developmental process in the management of manufacturing and chain production. The term also applies to the fourth industrial revolution. It represents a significant transformation regarding the way we produce products by the digitisation of manufacturing and a new wave of technological change which is enabling factories and warehouses to transform. With software predicting maintenance needs before machinery breaks down, power docks and loading docks becoming intelligent and custom-designed parts produced on-demand- companies are harnessing the real potential of industry 4.0.

The term Industry 4.0 was first publicly introduced in 2011 as "Industrie 4.0" by experts from different fields such as business, politics, and academia under an initiative to enhance the German competitiveness in manufacturing. German federal government adopted the idea in 2020 for its High-Tech Strategy. From this, a Working Group was formed to further advise on the implementation of Industry 4.0.

An initiative 'Smart Manufacturing Leadership Co-alition' (SMLC) is working on the future of manufacturing which aims is to enable stakeholders in manufacturing industries to form collaborative R&D, implementation and advocacy groups for the development of approaches, standards, platforms and shared infrastructure that facilitate the broad adoption of manufacturing intelligence.[1]

In 2003, a set of recommendations was published describing smart machines, storage systems and production facilities capable of exchanging information autonomously, triggering actions and controlling each other independently. Facilitating fundamental improvements to industrial processes involved in manufacturing, engineering, material usage, supply chain and lifecycle management. The first industrial revolution which was the mechanisation through water and steam power, to mass-production and assembly lines using electricity in the second revolution. The fourth industrial revolution will revolutionise computers and automation and further enhance with smart and autonomous systems with data and machine learning, robotics, digital fabrication/additive manufacturing (3D printing), Internet 4.0, IoT, data analytics and blockchain.[2]

One key contributor to industry 4.0 is that conventional boundaries between sectors are eroding. It's becoming more difficult to tell the difference between companies and the relationships among suppliers, producers, and consumers with ever-evolving ecosystems. A new level of proficiency is required as new types of opportunities and challenges are notable for business and society at large. In Industry 3.0, computers were introduced and disrupted with the introduction of entirely new technology. As computers are connected and can communicate with one another without the need for human interaction, the future of Industry 4.0 will be a combination of cyber-physical systems, the Internet of Things and the Internet of Systems. As a result of the support of intelligent smart machines that can access data, factories will become more efficient and productive. The network of intelligent supply chains and machines that are digitally connected to create and share information will ultimately result in the prowess of Industry 4.0.

Industry 4.0 offers manufacturing companies the ability to streamline their services quickly and efficiently by knowing what needs attention in a timeframe that would be impossible for a human to do. Connected machines can process a tremendous volume of data to inform maintenance, performance and other issues, as well as analyse that data to identify patterns and insights.[3]

Smart connected machines can optimise logistics and supply chains by adjusting and accommodating when new information is present. Shipping yards are leveraging autonomous vehicles and equipment such as cranes and trucks to streamline operations with shipping containers. Robotics is being used in warehouses to support manufacturers by picking and shipping products. Additive manufacturing/3D printing technology is being used in production rather than just prototyping. Internet of Things helps internal operations, and through the use of the cloud environment where data is stored, equipment and processes become more optimised. While Industry 4.0 is still evolving companies who are adopting to technologies are also having to contend with how to upskill their current workforce to take on new work responsibilities made possible by Internet 4.0 and to recruit new employees with the right skills. In the near future, human workers and machines will work together seamlessly, complementing the other's efforts in a single loop of productivity. Deloitte UK research, suggests that despite inroads by digital and smart technologies in the workplace, essential "human" skills will remain relative for the foreseeable future. Given how traditional work, career, and HR models are, reorganising and reskilling workers around automation requirements for new ways of thinking about jobs, enterprise culture, technology, and, most importantly, people.[4]

Robots will gain enhanced senses, dexterity, and intelligence, thanks to accelerating advancements in machine vision, artificial intelligence, machine-to-machine communication, sensors, and actuators. They will become compact and adaptable, making it possible to deploy them safely alongside workers to program and interact. Such advances could make it practical to substitute robots for human labour in more manufacturing tasks, as well as service jobs, such as cleaning and maintenance.[5]

While the classic value chain often links together raw materials producers, manufacturers, distributors, and consumers through a well-established commercial infrastructure characterised by a stable set of transactions. The rise of digital technology allows individuals to connect outside of the value chain to deliver more efficient and useful products and services which leads to less importance of economies of scale and traditional divisions of labour. The costs of goods and services will be more liable to change, and relationships among companies will be more fluid with trustworthiness and a clear purpose business strategy among its people, suppliers, customers and regulators.

The biggest challenge of industrial leaders is not technology, rather it is people.[6] As digital technologies rapidly becoming a commodity, success largely depends on an organisation's Digital IQ, especially how well its digital leaders define, lead, and communicate transformations. It's also dependent upon digital qualifications of employees who need to roll out digital processes and services. Radical disruption isn't always comfortable for the people who make it happen, so change management will also be critical. And with data analytics becoming a core capability for every industrial company, enhancing skills and organisational structures will be critical.

Conclusion: Changes to value chains, products and services are on the horizon to satisfy customer demands. Products, systems and services will also be increasingly customised. Companies that can establish successful industrial platforms will have a significant advantage over competitors. Investing in the right technologies are essential and success or failure will depend on its people. Creating a digital culture, training digital natives and other employees, and having an active risk management and data integrity system in place as well as clear leadership is essential for working in a dynamic ecosystem environment for Industry 4.0.

Notes

Chapter One: The Third Wave Technology

1. Moeller, Leslie H., Nick Hodson, and Martina Sangin. 2017. "The Coming Wave Of Digital Disruption". Blog. *Strategy+Business*. https://www.strategy-business.com/article/The-Coming-Wave-of-Digital-Disruption.
2. Levy, Steven. 2016. "Steve Case Is Bullish On Tech's "Third Wave," Even If It's Kind of a Bummer". Blog. *Wired*. https://www.wired.com/2016/04/steve-case-is-bullish-on-techs-third-wave-even-if-its-kind-of-a-bummer/.
3. Teixeira, Thales S., and Peter Jamieson. 2014. "The Decoupling Effect Of Digital Disruptors". *Harvard Business School*. https://www.hbs.edu/faculty/Publication%20Files/15-031_accfb920-4667-4ccb-b2e1-453984a1879f.pdf.
4. Mulder, Jeroen. 2018. "Internet 4.0: Farewell To Digital Illiteracy". Blog. *Fujitsu*. https://blog.global.fujitsu.com/internet-4-0-farewell-to-digital-illiteracy/.
5. Louis, Tristan. 2017. "Internet 4.0: The Ambient Internet Is Here". Blog. *TNL.Net*. https://www.tnl.net/blog/2017/02/11/internet-4-0/.

NOTES

Chapter Two: Business Innovation

1. Laskowski, Nicole, and Margaret Rouse. 2017 "What Is SMAC (Social, Mobile, Analytics And Cloud)? - Definition From Whatis.Com". *Searchcio*. https://searchcio.techtarget.com/definition/SMAC-social-mobile-analytics-and-cloud.
2. Accelerate Your Transformation: Social, Mobile, And Analytics In The Cloud. 2017. Ebook. CapGemini Consulting. https://www.capgemini.com/wp-content/uploads/2017/07/cc_accelerate_your_transformation.pdf.
3. "New Technologies Will Drive ICT Spending Back To Double The Rate Of GDP Growth, According To IDC". 2017. IDC: The Premier Global Market Intelligence Company. https://www.idc.com/getdoc.jsp?containerId=prUS43163517.
4. "View Gartner's Nexus Of Forces". 2018. *Gartner*. https://www.gartner.com/technology/research/nexus-of-forces/.
5. "Open Platform 3.0™ Forum | The Open Group". 2018. Opengroup.Org. Accessed November 20. http://www.opengroup.org/membership/forums/platform3.
6. Dave, Rishi. 2018. "In 2018, The Entire C-Suite Must Be Data-Savvy.". Blog. Adobe. Accessed November 20. https://www.adobe.com/insights/c-suite-must-be-data-savvy.html.
7. McCormick, James, Gene Leganza, and Jeremy Vale. 2018. "Build Digital Intelligence For Your Insights-Driven Business". Forrester.Com. https://www.forrester.com/report/Build+Digital+Intelligence+For+Your+InsightsDriven+Business/-/E-RES83961.
8. Vatash, Prateek. 2018. Digital Intelligence Briefing:

2018 Digital Trends. Ebook. https://wwwimages2.adobe.com/content/dam/acom/au/landing/DT18/Econsultancy-2018-Digital-Trends.pdf.

9 Hall, Bryce, Tanguy Catlin, Jacques Bughin, and Nicolas Van Zeebroeck. 2017. "Improving Your Digital Intelligence". MIT Sloan Management Review. https://sloanreview.mit.edu/article/improving-your-digital-intelligence/.

Chapter Three: Change Management

1 Millennials At Work Reshaping The Workplace. 2018. Ebook. PwC. Accessed November 21. https://www.pwc.com/co/es/publicaciones/assets/millennials-at-work.pdf.

2 Alton, Larry. 2017. "5 Ways Millennials Will Transform The Workplace In 2018". Blog. Forbes. https://www.forbes.com/sites/larryalton/2017/12/28/5-ways-millennials-will-transform-the-workplace-in-2018/#24224295558d.

3 The 2016 Deloitte Millennial Survey Winning Over The Next Generation Of Leaders. 2016. Ebook. Deloitte.https://www2.deloitte.com/content/dam/Deloitte/global/Documents/About-Deloitte/gx-millenial-survey-2016-exec-summary.pdf.

4 Dholakiya, Pratik. 2016. "4 Reasons To Embrace Millennial Values In Change Management". Blog. Entrepreneur Europe. https://www.entrepreneur.com/article/271741.

5 Millennials At Work Reshaping The Workplace. 2018. Ebook. PwC. Accessed November 21. https://www.pwc.com/co/es/publicaciones/assets/millennials-at-work.pdf.

6 Monych, Bonnie. 2018. "Millennials In Charge: How They're Changing The Workplace". Blog. Insperity. Accessed November 21.

NOTES

      https://www.insperity.com/blog/millennials-in-charge-how-theyre-changing-the-workplace/.

7   Taylor, Kate. 2014. "Want To Reach Millennials? This Is How They Spend Their Time. (Infographic)". Blog. Entrepreneur Europe. https://www.entrepreneur.com/article/238294.

8   Merchant, Vaqar, Divya Jyoti Behl, Abhay Raina, and Supriya Sawant. 2018. "Managing Change For A Millennial Workforce". Capital H Blog. https://capitalhblog.deloitte.com/2018/04/25/managing-change-for-a-millennial-workforce/.

Chapter Four: Digital Leadership

1   "The Role Of The CMO Is Evolving And Has Transformed Faster Than Any Other". 2018. Blog. Deloitte Canada. Accessed November 21. https://www2.deloitte.com/ca/en/pages/chief-marketing-officer/articles/the-evolving-role-of-the-cmo.html.

2   Barta, Thomas, and Patrick Barwise. 2017. "Why Effective Leaders Must Manage Up, Down, And Sideways". Mckinsey & Company. https://www.mckinsey.com/featured-insights/leadership/why-effective-leaders-must-manage-up-down-and-sideways.

3   School, IESE. 2013. "How To Be A Digital Leader". Forbes. https://www.forbes.com/sites/iese/2013/08/23/how-to-be-a-digital-leader/#46bcb0495a6e.

4   "5 Habits Of Truly Disruptive Leaders". 2015. Fast Company. https://www.fastcompany.com/3052725/5-habits-of-truly-disruptive-leaders.

5   "How To Be A Digital Leader". 2013. Blog. *Forbes*. https://www.forbes.com/sites/iese/2013/08/23/how-to-be-a-digital-leader/#5303adf55a6e.

6		Barter, Thomas and Barwise, Patrick. 2017. "Why Effective Leaders Must Manage Up, Down, And Sideways". Blog. *Mckinsey Quarterly*. https://www.mckinsey.com/featured-insights/leadership/why-effective-leaders-must-manage-up-down-and-sideways.
7		"The Role Of The CMO Is Evolving And Has Transformed Faster Than Any Other | Deloitte Canada". 2018. Deloitte Canada. Accessed November 21. https://www2.deloitte.com/ca/en/pages/chief-marketing-officer/articles/the-evolving-role-of-the-cmo.html.
8		"CMO-Mentum: Critical New Challenges Face Cmos". 2018. Deloitte Canada. Accessed November 21. https://www2.deloitte.com/ca/en/pages/chief-marketing-officer/articles/cmo-mentum.html.
9		Moorman, Professor. 2018. "How Does Your Marketing Budget Grow? – Key Trends From The CMO Survey". Blog. The CMO Survey. https://cmosurvey.org/2018/10/how-does-your-marketing-budget-grow-key-trends-from-the-cmo-survey/.

Chapter Five: Digital Marketing

1		"Digital Transformation". 2018. Digital Marketing Institute. Accessed November 22. https://digitalmarketinginstitute.com/business/digital-transformation.
2		Stephen, Andrew. 2017. "AI Is Changing Marketing As We Know It, And That's A Good Thing". Blog. Forbes. https://www.forbes.com/sites/andrewstephen/2017/10/30/ai-is-changing-marketing-as-we-know-it-and-thats-a-good-thing/.
3		Adams, Jennifer. 2018. "Global Marketing Automation

NOTES

    Spending Will Reach $25 Billion By 2023". Blog. Forrester. https://go.forrester.com/blogs/global-marketing-automation-spending-will-reach-25-billion-by-2023/.

4   "Forrester Data: Marketing Automation Technology Forecast, 2017 To 2023 (Global)". 2018. Forrester.Com. https://www.forrester.com/report/Forrester+Data+Marketing+Automation+Technology+Forecast+2017+To+2023+Global/-/E-RES143159.

5   "From Data To Disruption: Innovation Through Digital Intelligence - sponsored content from IBM". 2016. Harvard Business Review. https://hbr.org/sponsored/2016/12/from-data-to-disruption-innovation-through-digital-intelligence.

6   Infographics, MarTech. 2018. "What Is Martech Or Marketing Technology?". *Martech Today*. https://martechtoday.com/library/what-is-martech.

7   McBain, Jay. 2018. "Partner Relationship Management (PRM) Comes Of Age". Blog. *Forrester*. https://go.forrester.com/blogs/partner-relationship-management-prm-comes-of-age/.

8   "Do Brands Have Enough Martech Now?". 2018. Blog. *Marketing Charts*. https://www.marketingcharts.com/customer-centric/analytics-automated-and-martech-106003.

9   Bremmer, Michael. 2018. "What Tools Should Be In My Martech Stack?". Blog. *Marketing Insider Group: Content Marketing*. https://marketinginsidergroup.com/content-marketing/what-tools-should-be-in-my-martech-stack/.

10   Pemberton, Chris. 2017. "2017-2018 Gartner CMO Spend Survey". Blog. *Smarter With Gartner*. https://www.gartner.com/smarterwithgartner/2017-2018-gartner-cmo-spend-survey/.

Chapter Six: AI and Machine Learning

1. Gallagher, Kevin. 2018. "AI In Marketing: How Marketing Companies Can Leverage Machine Learning & Artificial Intelligence Tools For Advertising". Blog. *Business Insider*. https://www.businessinsider.com/ai-marketing-report-2018-3?IR=T.
2. Tweedie, Mitchell. 2018. "6 Technologies Behind AI". Blog. *Codebots*. https://codebots.com/ai-powered-bots/6-technologies-behind-ai.
3. Stephen, Andrew. 2017. "AI is changing marketing as we know it, and that's a good thing". Blog. *Forbes*. https://www.forbes.com/sites/andrewstephen/2017/10/30/ai-is-changing-marketing-as-we-know-it-and-thats-a-good-thing/#67434259dc40.
4. Alford, Jeff. 2018. "AI Marketing: What Does The Future Hold?". Blog. *Sas Insights*. Accessed November 12. https://www.sas.com/en_us/insights/articles/marketing/ai-marketing-what-does-the-future-hold.html.
5. Solis, Brian. 2017. "Extreme Personalization Is The New Personalization: How To Use AI To Personalize Consumer Engagement". Blog. *Forbes*. https://www.forbes.com/sites/briansolis/2017/11/30/extreme-personalization-is-the-new-personalization-how-to-use-ai-to-personalize-consumer-engagement/#70ec2017829a.
6. Tjepkema, Lindsay. 2018. "Introducing The AI-Driven Marketer: Here'S How Marketing Is Evolving In 2018 And Beyond". Blog. *Emarsys*. Accessed November 13. https://www.emarsys.com/en-uk/resources/blog/introducing-ai-driven-marketer-how-marketing-evolving-2018-beyond/.

NOTES

Chapter Seven: Business Value of APIs

1. "API Strategy For Business". 2018. Mulesoft. Accessed November 22. https://www.mulesoft.com/resources/api/connected-business-strategy.
2. Pettey, Christy. 2017. "Put Apis At The Center Of Your Digital Business Platform". Blog. Smarter With Gartner. https://www.gartner.com/smarterwithgartner/put-apis-at-the-center-of-your-digital-business-platform/.
3. "Digital Business Ecosystems & The Platform Economy". 2018. Gartner. Accessed November 22. https://www.gartner.com/technology/topics/business-ecosystems.jsp.
4. Columbus, Louis. 2017. "2017 Is Quickly Becoming The Year Of The API Economy". Blog. Forbes. https://www.forbes.com/sites/louiscolumbus/2017/01/29/2017-is-quickly-becoming-the-year-of-the-api-economy/#4b2927256a41.
5. "Legacy System Integration". 2018. Mulesoft. Accessed November 22. https://www.mulesoft.com/resources/esb/legacy-system-integration.
6. Ramadath, Srinivas, Keerthi Iyengar, Daniel Stephens, and Somesh Khanna. 2017. "What It Really Takes To Capture The Value Of Apis". Mckinsey & Company. https://www.mckinsey.com/business-functions/digital-mckinsey/our-insights/what-it-really-takes-to-capture-the-value-of-apis.

Chapter Eight: Digital Transformation

1. "Insights & Data Strategy". 2018. *Capgemini US*. Accessed November 14. https://www.capgemini.com/us-en/service/digital-

2. *The age of analytics: Competing in a data driven world.* 2016. Ebook. McKinsey Global Institute. https://www.mckinsey.com/~/media/McKinsey/Business%20Functions/McKinsey%20Analytics/Our%20Insights/The%20age%20of%20analytics%20Competing%20in%20a%20data%20driven%20world/MGI-The-Age-of-Analytics-Full-report.ashx.
3. Isern, Josep, and Caroline Pung. 2007. "Driving Radical Change". Mckinsey & Company. https://www.mckinsey.com/business-functions/organization/our-insights/driving-radical-change.
4. D. Evans, Nicholas. 2015. "6 Steps For Digital Transformation". Blog. CIO From IDG. https://www.cio.com/article/2988012/it-management/6-steps-for-digital-transformation.html.
5. Saliunas, J. (2007). Transformation program management. Paper presented at PMI® Global Congress 2007—North America, Atlanta, GA. Newtown Square, PA: Project Management Institute.
6. Chiles, Jaret. 2017. "Untangling Transformation: IT Vs. Digital Vs. Business". Blog. *Rackspace.* https://blog.rackspace.com/untangling-transformation-it-digital-business.
7. Westerman, George. Bonnet, Didier. McAfee, Andrew. 2014. "The Nine Elements Of Digital Transformation". Blog. *MIT Sloan Management Review.* https://sloanreview.mit.edu/article/the-nine-elements-of-digital-transformation/.
8. "Digitization, Digitalization And Digital Transformation: The Differences". 2019. *I-SCOOP.* Accessed February 22. https://www.i-scoop.eu/digitization-digitalization-digital-transformation-disruption/.
9. Baculard, Laurent-Pierre. 2017. "To Lead A Digital

NOTES

Transformation, Ceos Must Prioritize". Blog. *Harvard Business Review.* https://hbr.org/2017/01/to-lead-a-digital-transformation-ceos-must-prioritize.

10   *Digital Enablement Turning Your Transformation Into A Successful Journey.* 2019. Ebook. Deloitte. Accessed February 22. https://www2.deloitte.com/content/dam/Deloitte/ie/Documents/Technology/IE_C_HC_campaign.pdf.

11   "Five Pillars Of Digital Transformation: Skills And Talent Management". 2017. *Digitalistmag.Com.* https://www.digitalistmag.com/future-of-work/2017/06/08/5-pillars-of-digital-transformation-skills-and-talent-management-05143666.

12   Smith, Eileen. 2018. "Worldwide Spending On Digital Transformation Will Be Nearly $2 Trillion In 2022 As Organizations Commit To DX, According To A New IDC Spending Guide". Blog. *IDC Media Center.* https://www.idc.com/getdoc.jsp?containerId=prUS44440318.

13   Murray, Sarah. 2018. "As Global Leader In Digital Transformation Market Research, IDC Reveals Worldwide Digital Transformation Predictions". Blog. *IDC Media Center.* https://www.idc.com/getdoc.jsp?containerId=prUS44430918.

14   "Sana'S Digital Transformation And B2B E-Commerce Report 2018-19". 2018. *Sana Commerce.* https://www.sana-commerce.com/us/digital-transformation-and-b2b-e-commerce-report/.

Chapter Nine: Emerging Technologies

1   *The Next Era Of Human|Machine Partnerships.* 2017. Ebook. IFTF. https://www.delltechnologies.com/content/dam/delltechnologies/assets/perspectives/2030/pdf/SR1940_IFTFf

orDellTechnologies_Human-Machine_070517_readerhigh-res.pdf.
2. Panetta, Kasey. 2018. "Gartner Top 10 Strategic Technology Trends For 2019". *Gartner.Com.* https://www.gartner.com/smarterwithgartner/gartner-top-10-strategic-technology-trends-for-2019/.

Chapter Ten: Customer Experience

1. Rinke, Alexander. 2018. "How Digital Transformation Can Help Cultivate Customer Experiences". Blog. Forbes. https://www.forbes.com/sites/forbestechcouncil/2018/09/24/how-digital-transformation-can-help-cultivate-customer-experiences/.
2. Clark, Tim. 2017. "New Research Finds Customer Experience At The Heart Of Digital Transformation". Blog. Forbes. https://www.forbes.com/sites/sap/2017/07/13/why-digital-leaders-focus-on-customer-experience/#2ae58bb96228.
3. Maechler, Nicolas, Robert Park, and Kevin Neher. 2016. "From Touchpoints To Journeys: Seeing The World As Customers Do". Mckinsey & Company. https://www.mckinsey.com/business-functions/marketing-and-sales/our-insights/from-touchpoints-to-journeys-seeing-the-world-as-customers-do.
4. Solis, Brian. 2018. "The 2017 State Of Digital Transformation | Altimeter, A Prophet Company". Marketing.Prophet.Com. Accessed November 23. https://marketing.prophet.com/acton/media/33865/altimeter--the-2017-state-of-digital-transformation.

NOTES

Chapter Eleven: Workforce Evolution

1. Keller, Scott, and Mary Meaney. 2017. "Attracting And Retaining The Right Talent". Mckinsey & Company.https://www.mckinsey.com/business-functions/organization/our-insights/attracting-and-retaining-the-right-talent.
2. Meister, Jeanne. 2017. "The Employee Experience Is The Future Of Work: 10 HR Trends For 2017". Blog. Forbes. https://www.forbes.com/sites/jeannemeister/2017/01/05/the-employee-experience-is-the-future-of-work-10-hr-trends-for-2017/#7088c06620a6.
3. Bersin, Josh. 2016. "New Research Shows Why Focus On Teams, Not Just Leaders, Is Key To Business Performance". Blog. Forbes.https://www.forbes.com/sites/joshbersin/2016/03/03/why-a-focus-on-teams-not-just-leaders-is-the-secret-to-business-performance/#2c7e736e24d5.
4. "New Survey Explores The Changing Landscape Of Teamwork - Microsoft 365 Blog". 2018. Microsoft 365 Blog. https://www.microsoft.com/en-us/microsoft-365/blog/2018/04/19/new-survey-explores-the-changing-landscape-of-teamwork/.
5. Savitz, Eric. 2012. "The Empowered Employee Is Coming; Is The World Ready?". Blog. Forbes. https://www.forbes.com/sites/ciocentral/2012/02/09/the-empowered-employee-is-coming-is-the-world-ready/#15ec050449b8.
6. Bersin, Josh. 2017. "HR Technology For 2018: Ten Disruptions Ahead". Blog. Forbes. https://www.forbes.com/sites/joshbersin/2017/11/02/hr-technology-for-2018-ten-disruptions-ahead/#b57ed2243b75.
7. "Press Detail". 2016. Kornferry.Com. https://www.kornferry.com/press/korn-ferry-hay-

	group-global-study-driving-culture-change-key-leadership-priority.
8	Roberts, Stephanie. 2018. "The Advantages Of A Remote Workforce". Blog. Forbes. https://www.forbes.com/sites/forbestechcouncil/2018/08/23/the-advantages-of-a-remote-workforce/#5b8f07d67b0d.
9	Fries, Laura. 2017. "Today'S CHRO – The Newest Data-Driven C-Suite Executive". Blog. *The Business Journals*. https://www.bizjournals.com/bizjournals/how-to/human-resources/2017/01/today-s-chro-the-newest-data-driven-c-suite.html.
10	"Make Your CEO Invest In HR Technology Today". 2017. Blog. *HR Technologist*. https://www.hrtechnologist.com/articles/performance-management-hcm/make-your-ceo-invest-in-hr-technology-today/.
11	2018 HR Technology Disruptions: Productivity, Design & Intelligence Reign. 2018. Ebook. Deloitte. https://www2.deloitte.com/content/dam/Deloitte/us/Documents/human-capital/us-hc-2018-hr-technology-disruptions.pdf.
12	Bersin, Josh. 2018. HR Technology Disruptions For 2018 Productivity, Design, And Intelligence Reign. Ebook. Bersin. http://marketing.bersin.com/rs/976-LMP-699/images/HRTechDisruptions2018-Report-100517.pdf.

Chapter Twelve: Fourth Industrial Revolution

1	Gandhi, Nirjar. 2015. "Industry 4.0 – Fourth Industrial Revolution". Blog. SAP. https://blogs.sap.com/2015/06/30/industry-40-fourth-industrial-revolution/.
2	Marr, Bernard. 2018. "What Is Industry 4.0? Here's A

NOTES

    Super Easy Explanation For Anyone". Blog. *Forbes.* https://www.forbes.com/sites/bernardmarr/2018/09/02/what-is-industry-4-0-heres-a-super-easy-explanation-for-anyone/#1e4f8d1b9788.

3   Schwieters, Norbert, and Bob Moritz. 2017. "10 Principles For Leading The Next Industrial Revolution". Strategy+Business. https://www.strategy-business.com/article/10-Principles-for-Leading-the-Next-Industrial-Revolution?gko=f73d3.

4   Abbatiello, Anthony, Tim Boehm, Jeff Schwartz, and Sharon Chand. 2018. "No-Collar Workforce: Humans And Machines In One Loop—Collaborating In Roles And New Talent Models". *Deloitte Insights.* https://www2.deloitte.com/insights/us/en/focus/tech-trends/2018/no-collar-workforce.html.

5   *Disruptive Technologies: Advances That Will Transform Life, Business, And The Global Economy.* 2013. Ebook. McKinsey Global Institute. https://www.mckinsey.com/~/media/McKinsey/Business%20Functions/McKinsey%20Digital/Our%20Insights/Disruptive%20technologies/MGI_Disruptive_technologies_Full_report_May2013.ashx.

6   "Industry 4.0: Building The Digital Enterprise". 2016. Pwc.Com. https://www.pwc.com/gx/en/industries/industries-4.0/landing-page/industry-4.0-building-your-digital-enterprise-april-2016.pdf.

Bibliography

"5 Habits Of Truly Disruptive Leaders". 2015. Fast Company. https://www.fastcompany.com/3052725/5-habits-of-truly-disruptive-leaders.

"API Strategy For Business". 2018. Mulesoft. Accessed November 22. https://www.mulesoft.com/resources/api/connected-business-strategy.

"CMO-Mentum: Critical New Challenges Face Cmos". 2018. Deloitte Canada. Accessed November 21. https://www2.deloitte.com/ca/en/pages/chief-marketing-officer/articles/cmo-mentum.html.

"Digital Business Ecosystems & The Platform Economy". 2018. Gartner. Accessed November 22. https://www.gartner.com/technology/topics/business-ecosystems.jsp.

"Digital Transformation". 2018. Digital Marketing Institute. Accessed November 22. https://digitalmarketinginstitute.com/business/digital-transformation.

"Digitization, Digitalization And Digital Transformation: The Differences". 2019. *I-SCOOP*. Accessed February 22. https://www.i-scoop.eu/digitization-digitalization-digital-transformation-disruption/.

NOTES

"Do Brands Have Enough Martech Now?". 2018. Blog. *Marketing Charts*. https://www.marketingcharts.com/customer-centric/analytics-automated-and-martech-106003.

"Five Pillars Of Digital Transformation: Skills And Talent Management". 2017. *Digitalistmag.Com*. https://www.digitalistmag.com/future-of-work/2017/06/08/5-pillars-of-digital-transformation-skills-and-talent-management-05143666.

"Forrester Data: Marketing Automation Technology Forecast, 2017 To 2023 (Global)". 2018. Forrester.Com. https://www.forrester.com/report/Forrester+Data+Marketing+Automation+Technology+Forecast+2017+To+2023+Global/-/E-RES143159.

"From Data To Disruption: Innovation Through Digital Intelligence - sponsored content from IBM". 2016. Harvard Business Review. https://hbr.org/sponsored/2016/12/from-data-to-disruption-innovation-through-digital-intelligence.

"How To Be A Digital Leader". 2013. Blog. *Forbes*. https://www.forbes.com/sites/iese/2013/08/23/how-to-be-a-digital-leader/#5303adf55a6e.

"Industry 4.0: Building The Digital Enterprise". 2016. Pwc.Com. https://www.pwc.com/gx/en/industries/industries-4.0/landing-page/industry-4.0-building-your-digital-enterprise-april-2016.pdf.

"Insights & Data Strategy". 2018. *Capgemini US*. Accessed November 14. https://www.capgemini.com/us-en/service/digital-services/insights-data-2/insights-data-strategy/.

"Legacy System Integration". 2018. Mulesoft. Accessed November 22. https://www.mulesoft.com/resources/esb/legacy-system-integration.

"Make Your CEO Invest In HR Technology Today". 2017. Blog. *HR Technologist*. https://www.hrtechnologist.com/articles/performance-management-hcm/make-your-ceo-invest-in-hr-technology-today/.

"New Survey Explores The Changing Landscape Of Teamwork - Microsoft 365 Blog". 2018. Microsoft 365 Blog. https://www.microsoft.com/en-us/microsoft-365/blog/2018/04/19/new-survey-explores-the-changing-landscape-of-teamwork/.

"New Technologies Will Drive ICT Spending Back To Double The Rate Of GDP Growth, According To IDC". 2017. IDC: The Premier Global Market Intelligence Company. https://www.idc.com/getdoc.jsp?containerId=prUS43163517.

"Open Platform 3.0™ Forum | The Open Group". 2018. Opengroup.Org. Accessed November 20. http://www.opengroup.org/membership/forums/platform3.

"Press Detail". 2016. Kornferry.Com. https://www.kornferry.com/press/korn-ferry-hay-group-global-study-driving-culture-change-key-leadership-priority.

"The Role Of The CMO Is Evolving And Has Transformed Faster Than Any Other". 2018. Blog. Deloitte Canada. Accessed November 21. https://www2.deloitte.com/ca/en/pages/chief-marketing-officer/articles/the-evolving-role-of-the-cmo.html.

"The Role Of The CMO Is Evolving And Has Transformed Faster Than Any Other | Deloitte Canada". 2018. Deloitte Canada. Accessed November 21. https://www2.deloitte.com/ca/en/pages/chief-marketing-officer/articles/the-evolving-role-of-the-cmo.html.

"View Gartner's Nexus Of Forces". 2018. *Gartner*. https://www.gartner.com/technology/research/nexus-of-forces/.

NOTES

1 "Sana'S Digital Transformation And B2B E-Commerce Report 2018-19". 2018. *Sana Commerce*. https://www.sana-commerce.com/us/digital-transformation-and-b2b-e-commerce-report/.

1 Murray, Sarah. 2018. "As Global Leader In Digital Transformation Market Research, IDC Reveals Worldwide Digital Transformation Predictions". Blog. *IDC Media Center*. https://www.idc.com/getdoc.jsp?containerId=prUS44430918.

2018 HR Technology Disruptions: Productivity, Design & Intelligence Reign. 2018. Ebook. Deloitte. https://www2.deloitte.com/content/dam/Deloitte/us/Documents/human-capital/us-hc-2018-hr-technology-disruptions.pdf.

Abbatiello, Anthony, Tim Boehm, Jeff Schwartz, and Sharon Chand. 2018. "No-Collar Workforce: Humans And Machines In One Loop—Collaborating In Roles And New Talent Models". *Deloitte Insights*. https://www2.deloitte.com/insights/us/en/focus/tech-trends/2018/no-collar-workforce.html.

Accelerate Your Transformation: Social, Mobile, And Analytics In The Cloud. 2017. Ebook. CapGemini Consulting. https://www.capgemini.com/wp-content/uploads/2017/07/cc_accelerate_your_transformation.pdf.

Adams, Jennifer. 2018. "Global Marketing Automation Spending Will Reach $25 Billion By 2023". Blog. Forrester. https://go.forrester.com/blogs/global-marketing-automation-spending-will-reach-25-billion-by-2023/.

Alford, Jeff. 2018. "AI Marketing: What Does The Future Hold?". Blog. *Sas Insights*. Accessed November 12. https://www.sas.com/en_us/insights/articles/marketing/ai-marketing-what-does-the-future-hold.html.

Alton, Larry. 2017. "5 Ways Millennials Will Transform The Workplace In 2018". Blog. Forbes. https://www.forbes.com/sites/larryalton/2017/12/28/5-ways-millennials-will-transform-the-workplace-in-2018/#24224295558d.

Baculard, Laurent-Pierre. 2017. "To Lead A Digital Transformation, Ceos Must Prioritize". Blog. *Harvard Business Review*. https://hbr.org/2017/01/to-lead-a-digital-transformation-ceos-must-prioritize.

Barta, Thomas, and Patrick Barwise. 2017. "Why Effective Leaders Must Manage Up, Down, And Sideways". Mckinsey & Company. https://www.mckinsey.com/featured-insights/leadership/why-effective-leaders-must-manage-up-down-and-sideways.

Barter, Thomas and Barwise, Patrick. 2017. "Why Effective Leaders Must Manage Up, Down, And Sideways". Blog. *Mckinsey Quarterly*. https://www.mckinsey.com/featured-insights/leadership/why-effective-leaders-must-manage-up-down-and-sideways.

Bersin, Josh. 2016. "New Research Shows Why Focus On Teams, Not Just Leaders, Is Key To Business Performance". Blog. Forbes.https://www.forbes.com/sites/joshbersin/2016/03/03/why-a-focus-on-teams-not-just-leaders-is-the-secret-to-business-performance/#2c7e736e24d5.

Bersin, Josh. 2017. "HR Technology For 2018: Ten Disruptions Ahead". Blog. Forbes. https://www.forbes.com/sites/joshbersin/2017/11/02/hr-technology-for-2018-ten-disruptions-ahead/#b57ed2243b75.

Bersin, Josh. 2018. HR Technology Disruptions For 2018 Productivity, Design, And Intelligence Reign. Ebook. Bersin. http://marketing.bersin.com/rs/976-LMP-699/images/HRTechDisruptions2018-Report-100517.pdf.

NOTES

Bremmer, Michael. 2018. "What Tools Should Be In My Martech Stack?". Blog. *Marketing Insider Group: Content Marketing.* https://marketinginsidergroup.com/content-marketing/what-tools-should-be-in-my-martech-stack/.

Chiles, Jaret. 2017. "Untangling Transformation: IT Vs. Digital Vs. Business". Blog. *Rackspace.* https://blog.rackspace.com/untangling-transformation-it-digital-business.

Clark, Tim. 2017. "New Research Finds Customer Experience At The Heart Of Digital Transformation". Blog. Forbes. https://www.forbes.com/sites/sap/2017/07/13/why-digital-leaders-focus-on-customer-experience/#2ae58bb96228.

Columbus, Louis. 2017. "2017 Is Quickly Becoming The Year Of The API Economy". Blog. Forbes. https://www.forbes.com/sites/louiscolumbus/2017/01/29/2017-is-quickly-becoming-the-year-of-the-api-economy/#4b2927256a41.

D. Evans, Nicholas. 2015. "6 Steps For Digital Transformation". Blog. CIO From IDG. https://www.cio.com/article/2988012/it-management/6-steps-for-digital-transformation.html.

Dave, Rishi. 2018. "In 2018, The Entire C-Suite Must Be Data-Savvy.". Blog. Adobe. Accessed November 20. https://www.adobe.com/insights/c-suite-must-be-data-savvy.html.

Dholakiya, Pratik. 2016. "4 Reasons To Embrace Millennial Values In Change Management". Blog. Entrepreneur Europe. https://www.entrepreneur.com/article/271741.

Digital Enablement Turning Your Transformation Into A Successful Journey. 2019. Ebook. Deloitte. Accessed February 22. https://www2.deloitte.com/content/dam/Deloitte/ie/Documents/Technology/IE_C_HC_campaign.pdf.

Disruptive Technologies: Advances That Will Transform Life, Business, And The Global Economy. 2013. Ebook. McKinsey Global Institute. https://www.mckinsey.com/~/media/McKinsey/Business%20Functions/McKinsey%20Digital/Our%20Insights/Disruptive%20technologies/MGI_Disruptive_technologies_Full_report_May2013.ashx.

Fries, Laura. 2017. "Today'S CHRO – The Newest Data-Driven C-Suite Executive". Blog. *The Business Journals.* https://www.bizjournals.com/bizjournals/how-to/human-resources/2017/01/today-s-chro-the-newest-data-driven-c-suite.html.

Gallagher, Kevin. 2018. "AI In Marketing: How Marketing Companies Can Leverage Machine Learning & Artificial Intelligence Tools For Advertising". Blog. *Business Insider.* https://www.businessinsider.com/ai-marketing-report-2018-3?IR=T.

Gandhi, Nirjar. 2015. "Industry 4.0 – Fourth Industrial Revolution". Blog. SAP. https://blogs.sap.com/2015/06/30/industry-40-fourth-industrial-revolution/.

Hall, Bryce, Tanguy Catlin, Jacques Bughin, and Nicolas Van Zeebroeck. 2017. "Improving Your Digital Intelligence". MIT Sloan Management Review. https://sloanreview.mit.edu/article/improving-your-digital-intelligence/.

Infographics, MarTech. 2018. "What Is Martech Or Marketing Technology?". *Martech Today.* https://martechtoday.com/library/what-is-martech.

Isern, Josep, and Caroline Pung. 2007. "Driving Radical Change". Mckinsey & Company. https://www.mckinsey.com/business-functions/organization/our-insights/driving-radical-change.

NOTES

Keller, Scott, and Mary Meaney. 2017. "Attracting And Retaining The Right Talent". Mckinsey & Company.https://www.mckinsey.com/business-functions/organization/our-insights/attracting-and-retaining-the-right-talent.

Laskowski, Nicole, and Margaret Rouse. 2017 "What Is SMAC (Social, Mobile, Analytics And Cloud)? - Definition From Whatis.Com". *Searchcio*. https://searchcio.techtarget.com/definition/SMAC-social-mobile-analytics-and-cloud.

Levy, Steven. 2016. "Steve Case Is Bullish On Tech's "Third Wave," Even If It's Kind of a Bummer". Blog. *Wired*. https://www.wired.com/2016/04/steve-case-is-bullish-on-techs-third-wave-even-if-its-kind-of-a-bummer/.

Louis, Tristan. 2017. "Internet 4.0: The Ambient Internet Is Here". Blog. *TNL.Net*. https://www.tnl.net/blog/2017/02/11/internet-4-0/.

Maechler, Nicolas, Robert Park, and Kevin Neher. 2016. "From Touchpoints To Journeys: Seeing The World As Customers Do". Mckinsey & Company. https://www.mckinsey.com/business-functions/marketing-and-sales/our-insights/from-touchpoints-to-journeys-seeing-the-world-as-customers-do.

Marr, Bernard. 2018. "What Is Industry 4.0? Here's A Super Easy Explanation For Anyone". Blog. *Forbes*. https://www.forbes.com/sites/bernardmarr/2018/09/02/what-is-industry-4-0-heres-a-super-easy-explanation-for-anyone/#1e4f8d1b9788.

McBain, Jay. 2018. "Partner Relationship Management (PRM) Comes Of Age". Blog. *Forrester*. https://go.forrester.com/blogs/partner-relationship-management-prm-comes-of-age/.

McCormick, James, Gene Leganza, and Jeremy Vale. 2018. "Build Digital Intelligence For Your Insights-Driven Business". Forrester.Com.
https://www.forrester.com/report/Build+Digital+Intelligence+For+Your+InsightsDriven+Business/-/E-RES83961.

Meister, Jeanne. 2017. "The Employee Experience Is The Future Of Work: 10 HR Trends For 2017". Blog. Forbes.
https://www.forbes.com/sites/jeannemeister/2017/01/05/the-employee-experience-is-the-future-of-work-10-hr-trends-for-2017/#7088c06620a6.

Merchant, Vaqar, Divya Jyoti Behl, Abhay Raina, and Supriya Sawant. 2018. "Managing Change For A Millennial Workforce". Capital H Blog.
https://capitalhblog.deloitte.com/2018/04/25/managing-change-for-a-millennial-workforce/.

Millennials At Work Reshaping The Workplace. 2018. Ebook. PwC. Accessed November 21.
https://www.pwc.com/co/es/publicaciones/assets/millennials-at-work.pdf.

Millennials At Work Reshaping The Workplace. 2018. Ebook. PwC. Accessed November 21.
https://www.pwc.com/co/es/publicaciones/assets/millennials-at-work.pdf.

Moeller, Leslie H., Nick Hodson, and Martina Sangin. 2017. "The Coming Wave Of Digital Disruption". Blog. *Strategy+Business*.
https://www.strategy-business.com/article/The-Coming-Wave-of-Digital-Disruption.

Monych, Bonnie. 2018. "Millennials In Charge: How They're Changing The Workplace". Blog. Insperity. Accessed November 21. https://www.insperity.com/blog/millennials-in-charge-how-theyre-changing-the-workplace/.

Moorman, Professor. 2018. "How Does Your Marketing Budget Grow? – Key Trends From The CMO Survey". Blog. The CMO Survey. https://cmosurvey.org/2018/10/how-does-your-marketing-budget-grow-key-trends-from-the-cmo-survey/.

Mulder, Jeroen. 2018. "Internet 4.0: Farewell To Digital Illiteracy". Blog. *Fujitsu*. https://blog.global.fujitsu.com/internet-4-0-farewell-to-digital-illiteracy/.

Panetta, Kasey. 2018. "Gartner Top 10 Strategic Technology Trends For 2019". *Gartner.Com*. https://www.gartner.com/smarterwithgartner/gartner-top-10-strategic-technology-trends-for-2019/.

Pemberton, Chris. 2017. "2017-2018 Gartner CMO Spend Survey". Blog. *Smarter With Gartner*. https://www.gartner.com/smarterwithgartner/2017-2018-gartner-cmo-spend-survey/.

Pettey, Christy. 2017. "Put Apis At The Center Of Your Digital Business Platform". Blog. Smarter With Gartner. https://www.gartner.com/smarterwithgartner/put-apis-at-the-center-of-your-digital-business-platform/.

Ramadath, Srinivas, Keerthi Iyengar, Daniel Stephens, and Somesh Khanna. 2017. "What It Really Takes To Capture The Value Of Apis". Mckinsey & Company. https://www.mckinsey.com/business-functions/digital-mckinsey/our-insights/what-it-really-takes-to-capture-the-value-of-apis.

Rinke, Alexander. 2018. "How Digital Transformation Can Help Cultivate Customer Experiences". Blog. Forbes. https://www.forbes.com/sites/forbestechcouncil/2018/09/24/how-digital-transformation-can-help-cultivate-customer-experiences/.

Roberts, Stephanie. 2018. "The Advantages Of A Remote Workforce". Blog. Forbes. https://www.forbes.com/sites/forbestechcouncil/2018/08/23/the-advantages-of-a-remote-workforce/#5b8f07d67b0d.

Saliunas, J. (2007). Transformation program management. Paper presented at PMI® Global Congress 2007—North America, Atlanta, GA. Newtown Square, PA: Project Management Institute.

Savitz, Eric. 2012. "The Empowered Employee Is Coming; Is The World Ready?". Blog. Forbes. https://www.forbes.com/sites/ciocentral/2012/02/09/the-empowered-employee-is-coming-is-the-world-ready/#15ec050449b8.

School, IESE. 2013. "How To Be A Digital Leader". Forbes. https://www.forbes.com/sites/iese/2013/08/23/how-to-be-a-digital-leader/#46bcb0495a6e.

Schwieters, Norbert, and Bob Moritz. 2017. "10 Principles For Leading The Next Industrial Revolution". Strategy+Business. https://www.strategy-business.com/article/10-Principles-for-Leading-the-Next-Industrial-Revolution?gko=f73d3.

Smith, Eileen. 2018. "Worldwide Spending On Digital Transformation Will Be Nearly $2 Trillion In 2022 As Organizations Commit To DX, According To A New IDC Spending Guide". Blog. *IDC Media Center.* https://www.idc.com/getdoc.jsp?containerId=prUS44440318.

Solis, Brian. 2017. "Extreme Personalization Is The New Personalization: How To Use AI To Personalize Consumer Engagement". Blog. *Forbes.* https://www.forbes.com/sites/briansolis/2017/11/30/extreme-

NOTES

personalization-is-the-new-personalization-how-to-use-ai-to-personalize-consumer-engagement/#70ec2017829a.

Solis, Brian. 2018. "The 2017 State Of Digital Transformation | Altimeter, A Prophet Company". Marketing.Prophet.Com. Accessed November 23. https://marketing.prophet.com/acton/media/33865/altimeter--the-2017-state-of-digital-transformation.

Stephen, Andrew. 2017. "AI Is Changing Marketing As We Know It, And That's A Good Thing". Blog. Forbes. https://www.forbes.com/sites/andrewstephen/2017/10/30/ai-is-changing-marketing-as-we-know-it-and-thats-a-good-thing/.

Stephen, Andrew. 2017. "AI is changing marketing as we know it, and that's a good thing". Blog. *Forbes*. https://www.forbes.com/sites/andrewstephen/2017/10/30/ai-is-changing-marketing-as-we-know-it-and-thats-a-good-thing/#67434259dc40.

Taylor, Kate. 2014. "Want To Reach Millennials? This Is How They Spend Their Time. (Infographic)". Blog. Entrepreneur Europe. https://www.entrepreneur.com/article/238294.

Teixeira, Thales S., and Peter Jamieson. 2014. "The Decoupling Effect Of Digital Disruptors". *Harvard Business School*. https://www.hbs.edu/faculty/Publication%20Files/15-031_accfb920-4667-4ccb-b2e1-453984a1879f.pdf.

The 2016 Deloitte Millennial Survey Winning Over The Next Generation Of Leaders. 2016. Ebook. Deloitte.https://www2.deloitte.com/content/dam/Deloitte/global/Documents/About-Deloitte/gx-millenial-survey-2016-exec-summary.pdf.

*The age of analytics: Competing in a data driven world.*2016.

Ebook. McKinsey Global Institute. https://www.mckinsey.com/~/media/McKinsey/Business%20Functions/McKinsey%20Analytics/Our%20Insights/The%20age%20of%20analytics%20Competing%20in%20a%20data%20driven%20world/MGI-The-Age-of-Analytics-Full-report.ashx.

The Next Era Of Human|Machine Partnerships. 2017. Ebook. IFTF. https://www.delltechnologies.com/content/dam/delltechnologies/assets/perspectives/2030/pdf/SR1940_IFTFforDellTechnologies_Human-Machine_070517_readerhigh-res.pdf.

Tjepkema, Lindsay. 2018. "Introducing The AI-Driven Marketer: Here'S How Marketing Is Evolving In 2018 And Beyond". Blog. *Emarsys*. Accessed November 13. https://www.emarsys.com/en-uk/resources/blog/introducing-ai-driven-marketer-how-marketing-evolving-2018-beyond/.

Tweedie, Mitchell. 2018. "6 Technologies Behind AI". Blog. *Codebots*. https://codebots.com/ai-powered-bots/6-technologies-behind-ai.

Vatash, Prateek. 2018. Digital Intelligence Briefing: 2018 Digital Trends. Ebook. https://wwwimages2.adobe.com/content/dam/acom/au/landing/DT18/Econsultancy-2018-Digital-Trends.pdf.

Westerman, George. Bonnet, Didier. McAfee, Andrew. 2014. "The Nine Elements Of Digital Transformation". Blog. *MIT Sloan Management Review*. https://sloanreview.mit.edu/article/the-nine-elements-of-digital-transformation/.

Note from the author:

Thank you for taking the time to read this book. I hope the contents of which has helped in some ways to better understand how technology is changing the way we live, work, purchase products, services and enjoy life experiences in our interconnected digital world. We are approaching the 4th industrial revolution and the 3rd wave of technology is causing industries to disrupt, workplaces to evolve and companies to transform. I shall certainly enjoy continuing to write on this subject matter and look forward to seeing how humans and machines will live and work together in the future.

kerryquinn.co.uk

info@kerryquinn.co.uk

Made in the USA
Las Vegas, NV
19 July 2021